Reflections of an Investigator

In Pursuit of Justice Book III

Reflections of an Investigator

Cover Design by Kent Hesselbein

© 2011 KGH Design Studio

http://www.kghdesignstudio.com/services.html

REFLECTIONS OF AN INVESTIGATOR

In Pursuit of Justice

Book III

Ron Cunningham

and Stan St. Clair

© 2011 by Ron Cunningham and Stan St. Clair, St. Clair Publications

All rights reserved. No part of this publication may be reproduced or transmitted in any form by any means electronic or mechanical, including telecopy, recording, or any information storage and retrieval system now known or invented, without permission in writing from the publisher, except by a reviewer who wishes to quote brief passages in connection with a review written for inclusion in a magazine, newspaper or broadcast.

ISBN 978-1-935786-18-4

Printed in the United States of America by

St. Clair Publications
P. O. Box 726
McMinnville, TN 37111-0726

http://stan.stclair.net

Note: some material is graphic and may not be suitable for young children.

Reflections of an Investigator

Table of Contents

Law Enforcement Code of Ethics	9
Current City Officials, Tullahoma, TN	11
Dedication	17
Photo: Memorial in Washington DC	21
In Acknowledgement of the Nursing Profession	22
Introduction	25
Chapter One	31
Chapter Two	35
Chapter Three	38
Chapter Four	43
Chapter Five	48
Chapter Six	54
Chapter Seven	61
Chapter Eight	65
Chapter Nine	68
Chapter Ten	74
Chapter Eleven	78

Reflections of an Investigator

Chapter Twelve	83
Chapter Thirteen	86
Chapter Fourteen	95
Chapter Fifteen	98
Chapter Sixteen	102
Chapter Seventeen	105
Chapter Eighteen	111
Chapter Nineteen	115
Chapter Twenty	122
Chapter Twenty-one	126
Chapter Twenty-two	129
Chapter Twenty-three	134
Chapter Twenty-four	137
Chapter Twenty-five	140
Photos: Two examples of MK graffiti	143
Chapter Twenty-six	144
Chapter Twenty-seven	148
Chapter Twenty-eight	152

Chapter Twenty-nine	155
Chapter Thirty	157
Chapter Thirty-one	159
Photo: Ron and Stan at book signing	161
Chapter Thirty-two	162
Chapter Thirty-three	171
Chapter Thirty-four	179
Chapter Thirty-five	188
Chapter Thirty-six	191
Chapter Thirty-seven	194
Chapter Thirty-eight	206
Chapter Thirty-nine	211
Chapter Forty	214
Chapter Forty-one	216
Photo: Lorraine Motel, Memphis, TN	218
Chapter Forty-two	219
Chapter Forty-three	225
Chapter forty-four	227

Pictorial (many photos)	229
History of Cunningham family	247
Photo: Entrance to Glengarnock Castle	250
Bibliography	251

Law Enforcement Code of Ethics

As a law enforcement officer, my fundamental duty is to serve mankind; to safeguard lives and property; to protect the innocent against deception, the weak against oppression or intimidation, and the peaceful against violence or disorder; and to respect the constitutional rights of all persons to liberty, equality and justice.

I will keep my private life unsullied as an example to all; maintain courageous calm in the face of danger, scorn or ridicule; develop self-restraint; and be constantly mindful of the welfare of others. Honest in thought and deed in both personal and official life. I will be exemplary in obeying the laws of the land and the regulations of my department. Whatever I see or hear of a confidential nature or that is confided to me in my official capacity will be kept ever secret unless revelation is necessary in the performance of my duty.

I will never act officiously or permit personal feelings, prejudices, animosities or friendships to influence my decisions. With no compromise for crime and with relentless prosecution of criminal, I will enforce the law courteously and appropriately without fear or favor, malice or ill will, never employing unnecessary force or violence and never accepting gratuities.

I recognize the badge of my office as a symbol of public faith, and I accept it as a public trust to be held so long as I am true to the ethics of the police service. I will constantly strive to achieve these objectives and ideals, dedicating myself before God to my chosen profession…law enforcement.

Current City Officials

Tullahoma, Tennessee

Lane Curlee, Mayor

Mayor **Lane Curlee** has a long history of public service in Tullahoma. He was first elected Alderman in 1982, serving a two-year term. In 1984 he was elected to the Tennessee General Assembly, where he served the 47th District (Coffee and Grundy Counties) for eight years before deciding not to seek re-election. In 1993 he was elected Mayor of Tullahoma, a position he served for nine years before deciding in 2002 not to seek re-election. In 2004 he ran for Alderman and served three years. In August 2011 he was elected to a three year term as the city's Mayor.

Curlee is a graduate of Tullahoma High School and MTSU, where he majored in Management and Finance. He and his wife, Evelyn, have been married 32 years and have two children, Rob, a MTSU graduate who lives in Murfreesboro, and Rosalyn, a student at Tennessee Tech in Cookeville. They have owned an advertising agency for 28 years and work for 20 clients in southern middle Tennessee.

Lane and Evelyn have been very active in Tullahoma, serving on many Boards and Agencies. In 2009 they formed Coffee County Cares 4 Families, an organization of volunteers that serves struggling families and foster children. They are members at the Church of Christ at Cedar Lane in Tullahoma.

Louis J. Baltz III

Louis J. Baltz III serves as **City Administrator** for the City of Tullahoma, Tennessee. Mr. Baltz was appointed to the position in January 1999. He has nearly thirty years of management experience in the public sector.

Mr. Baltz earned his Bachelor of Arts in Public Administration from Memphis State University in 1979. He is a 1992 graduate of the Senior Executive Institute of the University of Virginia. In 1995 he received his Master of Public Administration from Tennessee State University.

In the public sector he has held the positions of Director of Public Works and Assistant to the City Manager for the City of Brentwood, Tennessee. He serves as Vice-Chairman of the Tri-County Railroad Authority. He is the Chairman of the Coffee County Joint Economic and Community Development Board and is a member of the Franklin County Joint ECD Board. In addition, Mr. Baltz is vice-chair of the South Central Tennessee

Rural Transportation Authority Technical Committee.

He is a past president of the Tennessee Chapter of the American Society for Public Administration. Baltz is also a member of the International City Management Association, Arnold Community Council and Tullahoma Noon Rotary Club where he is a Paul Harris Fellow.

Mr. Baltz was recognized with the Distinguished Alumnus of the Year Award for 2008 by the Tennessee State University Institute of Government. In 2009 he was elected President of the Tennessee City Management Association and is a member of the Board of Directors of the Tennessee Municipal League.

He and his wife have three children.

Paul Blackwell

Paul Blackwell was appointed Tullahoma Chief of Police on June 4, 2007. Blackwell has been in law enforcement since February 1982. The Chief began his Law Enforcement career with the Norman Oklahoma Police Department. At Norman PD, Blackwell served as a Patrolman, Master Police Officer, and Criminal Investigator. Blackwell and family then re-located to Tampa Florida and served with the Hillsborough County Sheriff's Office as a Patrol Deputy. Blackwell and family moved to Coffee County in 1991 after returning from service with the military in the Gulf War. Immediately prior to the appointment as Chief, Blackwell served with the Coffee County Sheriff's Office for 14 years. During the time with the Sheriff's Office, Blackwell served as a Corrections Officer, Patrol Deputy, Jail Administrator, and Administrative Captain.

Blackwell has a Bachelor's Degree in Criminal Justice Administration from Middle Tennessee State University in Murfreesboro, TN, and a Masters Degree in Criminal Justice Management and Administration from Central Oklahoma State University in Edmond, OK. The Chief is a graduate of the 243rd session of the FBI National Academy

Blackwell served in the U. S. Marine Corps from 1974 – 1976 and in 2009 retired from the U. S. Army Reserves after a total of 25 years service. The Chief is a 2004 graduate of the U. S. Army Sergeant Major Academy. The Chief retired at the rank of Sergeant Major in the Military Police field.

The Chief is a member of the Tennessee Association Chiefs of Police, and the International Association Chiefs of Police. Blackwell is a 2001 graduate of the Coffee County Leadership Program. Blackwell and his family, wife Lenore and children Meghan and Jonathan, have lived in Tullahoma since 1992.

Dedication

To all of the law enforcement officers who lost their lives from January 1, 2011 to the beginning of the writing of this book.

See http://www.odmp.org/year.php.

A special dedication goes to the following **Tullahoma Police Department** officers who have passed from this life in the line of duty, in order of passing, most recent first.

Policeman Clifford Riddle

Tullahoma Police Department

End of watch: Thursday, January 1, 1987

Cause of death: Automobile accident

Date of Incident: January 1, 1970

Age 35

Policeman Riddle was severely injured in the head on collision on a two-lane highway headed back to Tullahoma after transporting a prisoner to Manchester. Policeman Henry Travis was killed instantly. Policeman Riddle was in a coma for 17 years until he died.

Officer Riddle had served with the agency for three years. He was survived by his wife, three children and six grandchildren.

Policeman Henry Travis

End of Watch: Thursday, January 1, 1970

Cause of death: Automobile accident

Age 49

Policeman Travis was killed in an automobile accident while returning from transporting a prisoner to Manchester. Policeman Clifford Riddle was severely injured in the same accident and was in a coma until his death.

Officer Travis had served the department for three years and was survived by his wife and two children.

Policeman James Flippo

End of watch: Tuesday, January 1, 1935

Cause of death: Gunfire

Age: Not listed

Policeman Flippo was shot and killed with his own weapon after a prisoner he was lodging attacked him and took his weapon.

Policeman E. C. Armstrong

Tullahoma Police Department

End of watch: Monday, December 10, 1934

Length of service: Not available

Cause of death: Gunfire

Age: Not available

Date of incident: December 3, 1934

Policeman Armstrong, Policeman Charles Holt and Policeman Lindsay Smith, of the Tullahoma Highway Patrol were shot and killed after responding to a domestic dispute.

Policeman Armstrong was the first officer to arrive at the scene and was shot by the drunk suspect, who opened fire with a .45 caliber hand gun. The first shot struck Policeman Armstrong's badge, and a second shot striking his spinal cord. Although wounded, he was able to return fire and struck the suspect in the arm.

The suspect fled to a nearby church, hiding in the crawlspace beneath the building. Policeman Holt and Patrolman Smith responded to the church and located the suspect. In an exchange of fire, Policeman Holt was fatally wounded. As the suspect came around the corner of the building, he shot Patrolman Smith twice, seriously wounding him. A second Highway Patrolman returned fire and killed the suspect.

Policeman Armstrong and Patrolman Smith were transported to Protestant Hospital where both succumbed to their wounds several days later.

Policeman Charles Holt

End of watch: Monday December 3, 1934

Length of service: Not available

Age: Not available

Cause of death: Gunfire

Date of incident: December 3, 1934

See above article on Policeman E. C. Armstrong.

Memorial in Washington, DC to Tullahoma's Fallen Officers

In Acknowledgement of the Nursing Profession

The law enforcement community, in general, owes a great debt of gratitude to the healthcare professionals who work alongside them in their care and dedication to the needs of humanity. The nursing profession is a great part of this fine group of public servants.

Nurses are healthcare professionals who, in union with others in their ranks, are greatly responsible for the treatment, well-being and recovery of, not only ill individuals, but the chemically dependent, and injured. Nurses perform a wide range of services, including treatment of life-threatening emergencies, administration of shots and other needed medications, and may also be involved in medical research.

Although she was not medically trained, Florence Nightingale was an early pioneer in both nursing and education, following her experiences in caring for the wounded British soldiers in the Crimean War (1853-1856) in Western Europe. Prior to this time, nursing was thought of as an occupation few common practices or standards. Nightingale's concepts and practices were used as a guide for establishing nursing schools at the nineteenth and

Reflections of an Investigator

the beginning of the twentieth century (See *Quaker to Catholic, Mary Howitt, the Lost Author of the Nineteenth Century* by Joy Dunicliff, St. Clair Publications, UK, USA, © 2010, page 73). This exuberant lady became a shining example of caring for and serving humanity; an example which shines today as brightly as it did in her day. This early hospital-based education is sometimes credited for the expansion of the nursing profession, now specialized and offered at post-secondary institutions.

Practice as a nurse is often defined by various governments. For example, the Canadian province of Ontario classifies nurses into Registered Practical Nurses, Registered Nurses (general class), and Registered Nurses (extended class). In this regard, the title nurse is protected by law within the province, and regulated by legislative statute. In the United States, nursing designations in general use are Registered Nurse, and Licensed Practical Nurse. The title which used to apply known as Nurses' Aid is now antiquated due to the need for more well-educated personnel. A qualified person now needs to undergo studies and qualify as a Certified Nursing Assistant, or CNA.

The higher the level needed for a role, the more education is required, of course. These professional men and women strive hard to give their patients a high level of care, and as such we applaud their valiant efforts.

Just as with physicians, nurses also can train for specialties. Some, for example, may prefer emergency room service (usually the first person seen by the patient is a nurse), while others prefer to serve in a doctor's office. Some prefer to deal with a particular sector of medical care, etc.

Wherever a dedicated nurse chooses to serve, their goal is to provide the highest level of professional care to their patients. A good nurse is the delight of any doctor.

I can tell you straight up, there is a nurse that is a delight to me. She is an RN (Registered Nurse), a BSN (Bachelor of Science in Nursing), a CEN (Certified Emergency Nurse), and an LMT (Licensed Massage Therapist). Her name is Linda Hudson Cunningham, and she is my wife.

Introduction

Ron has been an officer with the Tullahoma. Tennessee Police Department for the past twenty-six years, where he went to work two years after leaving his position as Sheriff of Moore County. He now serves as a captain over investigations. During this time, he has been involved in some extremely challenging cases, several of which we will bring out in this volume. In introduction, Ron would like to include a brief history of this fine city.

Tullahoma is in southern Middle Tennessee, primarily in lower Coffee County, but extending into Franklin County on its southeastern side. The population of Tullahoma proper was 17,994 in the 2000 census. The Tullahoma metropolitan area, however, includes Coffee, Franklin and Moore Counties, and is the second largest metropolitan area in land mass after the Capital metropolitan area, according to Wikipedia.

Tullahoma was founded in 1852 as a work camp along the new Nashville and Chattanooga Railroad. Its name was derived from a Choctaw word meaning "red rock." According to noted attorney, historian, author and editor, Sam Davis Elliott, in *Soldier of Tennessee,* however, Peter Decherd, who donated the land for the railroad right-of-way, was given the right to name the two stations along the line, naming one for himself, Decherd, and the other for his favorite horse, Tulkahoma, which was named for an Indian chief his grandfather had captured. Later the name was changed to Tullahoma.

Prior to the founding of Tullahoma and the building of the railroad, the area was settled by farmers who came mostly from Virginia and North Carolina. Early Settlers were Moore, Decherd, Anderson, Ragon, Montgomery, Ferrell, Stephenson, Gunn. A spring known to the first settlers as Bottle Spring, and later known as John Gunn's Spring, for an early settler from North Carolina who purchased the property in 1826, is today called Big Springs. This historic spring provided water for the steam locomotives according to Godspeed's *Historical and Biographical Sketches of Coffee County, Tennessee.*

Later, an extremely popular spa and resort was located a few short miles away between Tullahoma and Estill Springs, known as Oak Brook which was widely acclaimed for healing properties of the water containing sulfur and chalybeate. A hotel was built there in the late nineteenth century which came to accommodate up to 75 persons, with the five cottages on the property. Though smaller than some other Tennessee turn-of-the-century resorts, activities included tennis, bowling, swimming, boating, fishing, horseback riding and ballroom dancing, The Oak Brook Hotel and Resort remained open into the mid-twentieth century.

In 2009 I was privileged to visit at length with the Oak Brook property's owner, Johnny Mitchell, who purchased it upon it's closing to the public in the 1950s. During our parlay, Mr. Mitchell related to me a great deal of the history of the property, which was on what he called "the Old Dixie Road." He told me that people came from as far away as Europe to stay at the resort in the late 1800s. The property is over one hundred acres, and borders Tim's Ford Lake.

Another Tullahoma area resort frequented by international groups during this era was Cascade Falls Resort. Both the Oak Brook and Cascade Falls resorts are featured on the Tennessee State Library and Archives website, and were listed in the *State of Tennessee Board of Health Bulletin, Volume 5*, published in Nashville on November 20, 1889.

In April, 1861, Company B, 1st Regiment of Tennessee Volunteers formed Peter Turney's Division in Tullahoma, which joined Robert E. Lee's Army of Northern Virginia. This Division fought in the Battle of Bull Run, Fredericksburg, Chancellorsville, Gettysburg, and Petersburg, and surrendered to Ulysses S. Grant at Appomattox.

Reflections of an Investigator

The town of Tullahoma became highly significant during the Civil War and served as the headquarters for the Confederate Army of Tennessee in 1863. The campaign of that year, which ultimately yielded control of Middle Tennessee to the Union and led to the eventual capture of Chattanooga, is known as the Tullahoma Campaign.

At the time of the war, Tullahoma was little more than a rough outpost, with no paved streets. 1863 was a rainy year in the area, and Tullahoma became known to soldiers on both sides as a place of perpetual mud. One witty Confederate officer in General Hardee's staff is said to have written his own view as to the origin of the town's name as being "'Tulla,' meaning mud, and 'Homa,' meaning more mud." General Braxton Bragg's selection of Tullahoma as the Confederate headquarters has been much criticized by military historians. In spite of its strategic location because of the railroad, it had no strong natural defenses, and little fortification at the time of occupation by the troops. Eventually it was abandoned with no battle.

Recovery was slow for Tullahoma after the war. But prosperity finally came due to the railroad link. During this time, it became renouned for its educational facilities, a rarity in those days. At the turn of the 20th century it became a popular health destination, with many spas around town. Manufacturing also grew up in the area, most notably, shoes, clothing and sporting goods. In 1924, the General Store Corporation was established there, which would eventually become Genesco, Inc., a diversified apparel firm, the oldest listed Tennessee member of the New York Stock Exchange. Since the early 1900s a variety of sports products have been manufactured in Tullahoma. These include baseballs, bats and golf clubs by Campbell Manufacturing, Wilson, Worth Sports, and Rawlings. In 1939, US Highway 41A was built through town, giving Tullahoma direct auto access to Nashville and Chattanooga.

The area is also famous for whisky. George Dickel has its roots in Tullahoma, while Jack Daniel's is distilled only 12 miles to the southwest in neighboring Lynchburg, Moore County.

In the early-to-mid-20th century, the area benefitted from considerable federal investment and development. This derived from the TVA (Tennessee Valley Authority) and the establishment of Camp Forest, an infantry training center and POW camp, and continues today with Arnold Engineering and Development Center (AEDC), where the Air Force and NASA did early wind tunnel testing. Later, the state located two significant institutions of higher learning there, Motlow State Community College, and the University of Tennessee's Space Institute.

Ron and I were pleased to present the first book of this series, *Conspiracy in the Town that Time Forgot* to be purchased through the bookstores at two locations of Motlow as a tool for students of the Criminal Justice System. It was very well received, for which we are grateful.

Today, manufacturing is a smaller part of Tullahoma's economy. The town's growth has been slow, but constant, due to a combination of local institutions of higher learning, tourism, manufacturing and retail. The presence of AEDC and the Space Institute and its proximity to the U.S. Space and Rocket Center in Huntsville, Alabama has spawned a small aeronautical industry in the area.

Tullahoma has, thus, made headlines through the years of Ron's tenure a number of times. I invite the reader to join in the adventure which Ron calls *Reflections of an Investigator*.

This volume is based on actual cases with which Ron has been involved while serving on the force in Tullahoma. Dates, names, and some details have been altered for effect, flow and drama. I want to thank Ron for allowing me the license to *"use my imagination to put words onto paper."* - Stan St. Clair

Chapter One

An orange-colored haze rested on the mountainous eastern horizon, proudly signaling the dawn. The thin morning light grew warmer, sunnier, as I slipped out of bed.

I'd like mornings a lot better if they started later. I usually have a couple of cups of coffee before leaving for work, but it was later than usual, so I got dressed quickly, kissed my wife good-bye, rushed out to my vehicle, and headed for the office and a brand new day. When I arrived, of course I the first thing I did was perk a pot of coffee and sit down at my desk with a fresh, hot cup of the irresistible stuff.

It was September 23, 2010. I began my daily routine by turning on my computer and checking in on the winsoms mobile cad system. As usual, I scanned the offence and incident reports from the evening and night before; then checked my voice-mail, facebook and e-mails. Joe Wells, a retired captain with the Memphis Police Department, and one of my best friends, who was now living in Tullahoma, usually e-mailed me some very interesting information. One particular article that morning caught my attention immediately. His note to me was, "I know you can relate to this. Thanks for all you have done and all you continue to do."

Reflections of an Investigator

You're not a cop until you taste them: *Author Unknown.*

The department was all astir. There was a lot of laughing and joking going on due to all the officers, myself included, preparing to hit the streets. As we sat in the squad room, we could barely sit still, anxiously awaiting assignments of our own portion of the city to serve and protect.

The sergeant had been with the department for longer than anyone could remember. And those years of service had made him into something of a legend.

The new guys, or rookies, as he called us, both respected and feared him. When he spoke, even the most seasoned officers paid attention. It was almost a privilege when one of the rookies got to be around when he would tell one of his police stories about the good old days. But we knew our place and never interrupted for fear of being reprimanded. He was respected and revered by all who knew him.

He would say, "So you want to be a policeman, do you, hero? I'll tell you what, when you can tell me what they taste like, then you can call yourself a real policeman."

I had heard this particular phrase dozens of times. We all had bets about 'what they taste like' actually referred to. Some believed it actually referred to the taste of your own blood after a hard fight. Others thought it referred to the taste of sweat after a long day's work.

One afternoon, I mustered up the courage and said, "You know, I think I paid my dues like everyone else, so what does that little saying of yours mean, anyway?"

He merely stated, "Well, seeing as how you've said and done it all, you tell me what it means, hero." He shook his head, snickered and walked away.

The next evening was to be the worst to date. The night started out slow, but as the evening wore on, the calls came more frequently and dangerous. I made several arrests and had a real nasty fight call. However, I was able to make the arrests without the suspects or myself being hurt.

I was looking forward to the end of the shift, and getting home before the girls left for school. I glanced at my watch and it was 5:55 A.M,, five more minutes before the shift was over. I don't know if it was fatigue or just my imagination, but as I was driving along on one of the streets on my beat on the way to the station, I thought I saw a little girl standing on a porch. After a second look there was a small child, a little girl about six or seven years old, standing on the porch holding an old rag doll dressed in what appeared to be an old tee shirt, hanging to her feet. I stopped to see what she was doing outside at that hour. I approached and knelt on the porch and asked her what she was doing outside by herself. She said her mommy and daddy got in a really big fight and now mommy won't wake up. The front door was standing open and as I approached and looked inside I could see a

Reflections of an Investigator

woman lying on the floor and a man was standing over her. He had blood on his hands and there was blood on the floor near the woman. I called for backup, pulled my duty weapon, kicked the door the rest of the way open and entered asking the male subject to to put his hands behind him. When he complied I approached and placed handcuffs on him. Backup arrived and I knelt to assist the woman. It was then I heard a small voice behind me. "Mr., please make my mommy wake up." The EMS arrived and took over. It was too late. She was gone.

I looked at the male subject, advised him of his rights and asked him what happened. He said he didn't know. "She was yelling at me to stop drinking and get a job. I had enough. I just shoved her so she would leave me alone. She fell and hit her head."

As I walked him out to my car in cuffs, I looked back at that little girl. Not only was I unable to wake her mommy, now I was taking away her daddy, too. Maybe if I had been just a little faster or done something different, maybe that little girl would still have a mommy. Tears began to fill my eyes.

I felt a large hand on my shoulder. I heard that all-to-familiar question, "Well, hero, what do they taste like?" Before I could get mad or even shout some sarcastic remark, I realized that all the emotions had flooded to the surface and a steady stream of tears were cascading down my face. It was at that moment I realized what the answer to his question was. Tears.

Reflections of an Investigator

He began to walk away. He stopped. "You know there was nothing you could have done differently. Sometimes you can do everything right and still the outcome is the same. Now you are a real policeman."

And God shall wipe away all tears from their eyes; and there shall be no more death, neither sorrow nor crying, neither shall there be any more pain: for the former things are passed away." (Revelation 21:4)

My eyes were fixated on the computer screen.

Yes, I could certainly relate — all too well. I began to reflect back over the tempestuous time when I, myself, was a rookie. The edifying years I spent as a deputy, and the horrid experiences I had when I almost lost my life. And how much I had grown since serving with the Police Department in Tullahoma. I only hoped that others could now respect me to some degree as the man in the story was revered.

That night at home, my mind had raced back to this thought-provoking email. It was then and there that I was to receive a call from the Chief of Police concerning a shocking triple murder which would shake the country — and the suspect, a 30-year-old Tullahoma Army recruiter, was holed up just down the street from my office. But we'll get back to that much later in this book.

Chapter Two

My mind took me tumbling back to those disquieting days that I would much rather have just forgotten. As atrocious as the experiences were while I had a contract out on my life, the two years between September 1982, when I left the Sheriff's Office in Lynchburg and August of 1984 were probably the worst of my life! I think I put in applications at every city and county law enforcement agency in Middle Tennessee. In August of '84 I was staying at the home of an acquaintance in Winchester, watching the kids while she was in Harton Hospital in Tullahoma. I had applied for a position as an officer with the Tullahoma Police Department. They were, of course, aware of the fact that I was working security for the hospital. When I arrived for work that night, I stopped by my friend's room to see how she was feeling. It was she who informed me that the Police Department was looking for me, as I had been selected for the open position.

On August 17th, 1984, I began my tenure at the Police Department in Tullahoma. Jack Welch was the Chief of Police at that time, Ron Darden was the City Administrator, and George Orr was the Mayor.

Reflections of an Investigator

To date I have had the honor of serving under four chiefs: Welch, Waggoner, Ferrell, and Blackwell. There have also been four city administrators: Ron Darden, Jana Vosika, Chuck Downham, and Jody Baltz. But during these years of my service, there have been seven mayors! The first was, as stated, George Orr, followed by Beth Bryant, Doyle Richardson, Joe Ervin, Lane Curlee, Steve Cope, Troy Bisby, and finally, Lane Curlee, again.

I spent the first thirty days on the day shift getting acquainted, and then I was required to transfer to the night shift, since I was the lowest man on the totem pole.

During that time on the day shift, I wrote citations and answered calls. Most of the calls were domestic related. Some were burglaries, traffic accidents, thefts, stolen vehicles, robberies, etc. You know — the every-day duties of an officer.

One humid, late August night, in my second year, I was patrolling with the air conditioner at full blast and the driver's side window down. I passed by the railroad trestle behind Builder's Supply, and out of the left side of my peripheral vision I saw something move under the trestle. I backed up to turn under the trestle, and there stood a white male, obviously shooting a needle into his arm. He made a dash to escape me as I gave chase on foot.

Reflections of an Investigator

My long legs enabled me to soon catch up to him. He swiftly turned toward me and stabbed the needle deep into my left hand. Fighting him with everything in me, I was finally able to secure the syringe, and clamp the cuffs on him. By the time I got him shoved into the back seat of my cruiser, behind the cage, my hand was in serious pain.

When I got him to the station, I locked him up in the bull pen. By this time, my hand was swollen about four times its normal size.

I drove myself to the emergency room, taking the syringe with me. When the doctor examined my hand and I related my story to him, he instructed the nurse to draw blood from the suspect. The specimen tested positive for Hepatitis, which was bad news for me, as I now needed gamma globulin, a weight-based injection of a medication consisting largely of Elmer's glue—this meant three shots in the buttocks. The nurse had tears in her eyes as she gave me the globulin, saying she didn't want to cause me any further pain.

As for the swelling in my hand, it was about a week before it started going down.

My hope for the reader is, "as you slide down the banister of life, may the splinters never point in the wrong direction."

Chapter Three

It was a hot, lazy evening in July a year or so later. I let the air slowly out of my pursed lips. I was pulling the second shift—two to ten.

J.C. Ferrell was Chief of Police, and David Allison was Patrol Captain. Tony Fuller was Patrol Sergeant. Scott Jackson, Ted Mooneyham, Tommy York and I were on patrol.

The Coffee County Communications Center dispatched a unit to the Tullahoma Village Apartments on a disturbance call at building five, upstairs. I answered the call and Ted backed me up. We both arrived on the scene at about the same time. There was a white male in faded blue jeans and a red polo shirt, appearing to be at least mildly intoxicated, perched on the upstairs landing.

Parking our patrol units, we both cautiously ascended the stairs. As we approached the landing, the subject sprinted frantically back inside his apartment. Then, standing just inside the door, he began cursing loudly, informing us that we couldn't touch him because he was inside his personal residence. With that, I reached into the room, grabbed his arm and pulled him outside.

"Not now, you're not!" I said in a tone which affirmed my unwavering position. "You're causing a disturbance. And as you know, we were in hot pursuit when you ran inside. You were already disturbing the peace before we got here!"

"You're under arrest!" Ted said, reaching out to cuff him.

Just then, the suspect aimed a right punch at Ted's nose. Ted jerked, and the suspect's fist barely grazed him.

Ted looked at me, his expression radiating his stunned feeling. "Did he just do what it *looked* like he did?"

"Yes, he sure did," I replied coolly. I wanted to smile, but couldn't bring myself to appear cavalier.

"Yes, I did," the brazen man agreed, throwing another powerful punch.

Both of us grabbed him this time, and the fight was on—all the way down the stairs and tumbling into the yard.

Suddenly Scott showed up, and all three of us were frantically trying to get the cuffs on him. Then, believe it or not, Captain Allison arrived and there were four of us wrestling with this devil-may-care drunk!

"Grab his arm and I'll put the cuffs on him!" Scott shouted above the rumble. The next thing I know, everyone grabs one of my arms and someone puts a cuff on me!

"Hey you guys! It's me you've got there!" I exploded. Now this wasn't a bit funny to me at the time.

Then a cuff went on the suspect and one of my arms was cuffed to one of his. That's the way it stayed until I got him to the station and into the bull-pen. Then the cuffs came off both of us. So goes the life of a policeman, never having a ghost of an idea what might happen next.

That weekend, Scott and I, and another of my other friends, along with our wives, rode our motorcycles up the winding mountain road to Fall Creek Falls State Park and back, stopping briefly to guzzle down some refreshment from a couple of gelid mountain springs. We took our sweet time sightseeing and enjoying the relaxing trek. We spent the full day getting our minds off of work and onto the beauty of our wondrous state.

Ron with friends at Fall Creek Falls

Chapter Four

It was *almost* good getting back to work after that weekend at Fall Creek Falls. At least I was in my comfort zone. Just as I was settling in and felt that things were getting a tad bit dull, one cool, rainy September morning we received a disturbing call stating that Larry Daggett III, a local construction worker, previously indicted and facing charges on six counts of statutory rape, had done it again! The mother had accused him of twice more having sex with her sixteen-year old daughter. The call had to be verified.

The dispatcher assigned me to the case. When I knocked on her door, the girl's mother was swift to open it. I dabbed the rain from my face with my folded handkerchief, wiped my sopped shoes on the rubber welcome mat, and sauntered on in.

The daughter was wearing light green shorts and a dingy white tee-shirt with a picture of Hank Williams, Jr. on the back, seated on a ragged flowered couch. Wiping tears from her eyes, her head was bowed, and her bleach-blonde hair dangling loosely about her slumped shoulders.

I glanced around the room, and saw nothing that would seem the least inviting to a teen. Drabness and a strong sense of insecurity seemed to be

Reflections of an Investigator

lurking through the house. A solitary faded Robert Frost fall landscape hung askew on the far wall.

The mother, however, was eager to spill her spiel into my attentive ears. Daggett, a suave, slick-talking forty-five year old, who had been released on a forty-thousand dollar bond, for an ongoing relationship with this same girl, had originally met her near a local country music bar, where she was hanging out with friends. Her single mother told me that was pushed at both ends trying to provide for her and her younger brother. She had grounded the daughter after it had gotten back to her that she had been meeting Daggett and leaving with him over a period of about three weeks earlier that year. She had just gotten the girl settled down—at least so she thought. It appeared to be a simple case of attention starvation, and I was tempted to feel sorry for everyone except the perp.

I took the lady's statement and asked the girl for her side of the story. I asked her if what her mother said was true. Had she really been seeing Daggett again?

"I'm in love with Larry," she said in a near whisper. Though I could barely discern the words, her intent was clear as crystal. We have all seen it a thousand times in law enforcement.

"You don't know the meaning of love! All you want is to get away from home!" The mother's voice was sharp, and the daughter dashed for her room, her sobs hanging in the air.

"Thank you, ma'am," I said, heading for the door.

Daggett was served with a summons to appear in Coffee County Circuit Court in Manchester for a preliminary hearing on October 28, and failed to show. The info was presented to Judge Gerald Ewell, Sr., who immediately issued a bench warrant for Daggett's arrest.

Again, I was elected, and took Tony Fuller as backup, heading to Daggett's apartment. Since it was another rainy day, and his employer was working on a roofing job, I figured that there was a good chance he was home. I was wrong.

After an APB, a tip was called in that Daggett was in neighboring Franklin County, and with the aid of Winchester Police Department, we located the apartment where he was staying.

After a crisp peck on the door, with no response, I spoke in a hearty tone. "Larry Daggett, Tullahoma Police Department! Open up!"

I had Tony guarding the rear entrance at a safe distance. Winchester Police were also on the scene. Sure enough, I heard Tony yelling as he exited at the rear. Dashing around the brick four-unit building on the nearest side, I saw that he had run in the opposite direction. A foot chase immediately ensued.

Finally, I reached the suspect slightly before Tony. He was trying to climb a chain-link fence. My gun glaring into his sadistic green eyes was enough. I grabbed his muscular right arm, pulling him off the fence, and Tony rushed in and got the cuffs on him.

Since the suspect was already out on a large bond, the judge was even tougher this go-round. It still took until mid-December to get the case before a judge. On Wednesday, December 17, Coffee County General Sessions Judge, Tim Brock, determined that "probable cause that a crime had been committed" existed to carry him over for trial, and bail was set on these offences at $750,000. Including surrender of the previous $40,000, the total bail was now $790,000. This was one of the highest bonds in Coffee County history.

When Daggett was scheduled to go to trial, he pled guilty. The charges were plea bargained to a total of four cases of statutory rape. He pled guilty to counts one and four, and the other two were then dismissed.

Daggett was sentenced to three years in prison, and community service. After serving one year he was placed on probation for the remaining two. During this probation, it was revoked and he ended up serving additional time.

But every day would be a new adventure which I could not begin to anticipate.

Chapter Five

It was another one of those sizzling, muggy midsummer's nights. No one at the station noticed that there was a full moon. Now there is an old saying, especially among law enforcement and the nursing profession that strange things happen during a full moon. That night everything became extremely busy—things *did* begin happening. On that particular evening that saying popped out at me like bread from the toaster.

I was Patrol Sergeant by this time, and my shift was 2:00 to 10:00. A call came through for a unit to investigate a naked woman streaking through the second floor of the Country Club Apartments. Officer Jennifer Grubs took the call, and I backed her up.

We both arrived on the scene at the same time and made a rush for the second floor. Upon our entry on that level, sure enough, there was a totally naked blonde lady about thirty years of age running up and down the hall, trying to get into any apartment which would let her in. She was both hysterical and intoxicated.

"Ma'am," I said in as calm a voice as I could muster, "where do you live?"

"My boyfriend and I got in a fight. He put me out in the hall without any clothes!"

She reminded me of a politician. No straight answer to my true concern. The lady's voice was a little slurred, but the message she was trying to convey was coming through loud and clear.

"Just calm down, ma'am," I said, but by now I wasn't any too calm myself. About that time a call came across our radio frequency. Someone on the south end of town was pleading for help. They needed all possible units to respond, and Officer Grubs left without further ado. There I was, alone with a hysterical naked woman!

"Ma'am, please tell me which apartment you live in."

She pointed, her hands still trembling.

I knocked on the door and no one came.

"Hello, sir." I said through the locked door, "I'm Sergeant Cunningham with the Tullahoma Police Department. Please open the door."

Nothing.

"Sir, if you don't open up at once, I'm going to kick this door down and take you to jail!"

The knob slowly turned, and I could see a man's hand undoing the chain on the safety latch.

"Ma'am," I told the naked lady, "please go inside and put some clothes on."

She dashed in and I stood there with my foot in the door until she came back.

"Now, listen, you two, I'm going now, but if we get another call on you folks tonight, you're both going to jail!"

I made a run for my cruiser, shaking my head, jumped in, and headed straight for the south end of town as fast as I could go.

When I arrived at the location on Cook Road, off of 41A, I had to stop because there were seven or eight people fighting in the middle of the road. I could hear the unmistakable voices of Captain Holder and Officer Caldwell calling for help.

All of a sudden, a car sped by with gunshots ringing out of it. It made a sharp turn and crashed into another auto parked on the side of Cook Road. The speeding car came to a halt with its nose at a 90 degree angle pointing toward the full moon. The occupants were attempting desperately to escape, but were unable to get out on their own.

"Throw your gun out first!" I yelled. "Then we'll help you guys out of there."

In the brightness of the moonlight, I saw the hand gun fly from the window, and we proceeded to aid them in their exit from the car. After they were out, I looked for my cruiser, and woefully realized that it was about two blocks away with the blue lights still flashing.

By this time, Manchester Police were also responding to the scene, along with the Sheriff's Department and State Troopers. They had attracted the entire Coffee County law enforcement community. In fact, Winchester, Eslill Springs and Franklin County had also arrived. But by this time there was an all-out riot going on in the road. I had to let my subjects go in order to respond to Captain Holder and Officer Caldwell. When we got to them they were standing back to back with their shotguns in their hands. We all backed up slowly as the other officers approached and we began arresting people left and right until we had ultimately gained control.

After the crowd dispersed, we left and went to Krystal's on North Jackson Street. Then the riot started up again, both inside and outside of Krystal, before we could get the perpetrators to the jail.

Reflections of an Investigator

Then the radio began squawking — the hospital was calling for help. Someone was trying to tear the doors off the E.R.

Finally, after the night shift came in early to be of assistance, and the day shift was recalled to help, along with Manchester, Coffee County S.O., Winchester, Estill Springs, Franklin County S.O. and the State Troopers, everything began to settle down. Regular calls started coming in and our shift had to stay late to catch up.

A disturbance call was received that a teenager was causing trouble at his parents' house. Officer Conway and I took that call.

When we went inside to confront the youth, he said sadistically, "They only sent two of you?"

My adrenaline was still kicked in from the riot. I told the smart aleck youngster that we were men enough to handle him and didn't need anyone else. I told him to get his tail off the couch and go get in the cruiser or I would personally put him there. He just looked at me, got up, and walked out to the cruiser without giving me any more lip. He was locked up in a juvenile detention center in Murfreesboro until his court date could be set.

I finally dragged in home, showered and flopped into bed for some much-needed rest! I was glad full moon wasn't but once a month.

Chapter Six

All of a sudden it started. One steamy Friday summer morning our office got a call that a car had been broken into and a radar detector and CB radio stolen. Of course our department did all we could to find the responsible party. I was assigned to the case and did all the normal stuff. I got with the vic and we dusted for fingerprints will no real success.

But little did I know that this would be only the beginning of a rash of car burglaries. First it would be on the east side, then on the west side of town. All sorts of sellable merchandise was being lifted — but always from autos. Stereos, car phones, jewelry — things like that — whatever the perps thought would bring enough to buy or trade for illegal substances. By this time, meth production was a major concern in our region, as it was in other areas around the state and the nation.

As I entered the pawn shop downtown, the bell over the door announced my presence and the proprietor looked up into my concerned eyes.

"Hey Ron, I would say 'Good to see you,' but I'm betting your not here to shoot the breeze."

"No, Jim, I'm not. We're having a rash of 'car jackin's,' as the kids say. There's been a bunch of stuff taken, and I need to check the list against your recent purchases.

"Okay...whatcha got there?"

"Let's see," I said, licking my thumb and turning the sheets on my notepad, "I'm looking for a combo tape deck and CD made by Panasonic. Serial number PA00154973-B9."

"Hold it, hold it! I don't have a photographic memory. Panasonic, you say? I think I had a Panasonic stereo come in last week. Let's see, I think I put it over here on a shelf...." Jim paused, yawned, and picked up the unit.

"Can you check this number," I said, handing him the notepad.

Jim reached in his pocket, removed a pair of brown plastic-rimmed reading glasses, and stuck them on his prodigious nose.

"Let's see," he said squinting, glancing back and forth from the notepad to the stereo player. "This number's a little hard to read. PA00...1549...73-B9, yep looks like it's a match! Dang! Sorry about this. It looks like I'm just up the creek on this one."

"How about a Fuzz-Buster?"

"Na, can't help you there."

Reflections of an Investigator

"Did this guy bring in any jewelry? I have several pieces of jewelry on this list." I said, half hoping he didn't have them. After all, Jim *was* my friend.

"Well....No...but I did get a nice cameo pin from another young fella a couple of weeks ago."

I frowned and looked at the list. "What color background?"

"I have it right here in the case," Jim said, opening the display with a flat key. "It's coral, as you can see, set in 10 karat gold."

"Well, it looks a heck of a lot like the picture I was given where the lady was wearing it. I'm afraid I'm gonna have to take it and let her ID it. Anything else that might be on our list? Electronics from cars, other jewelry?"

"Nope. That's all I bought from these two guys."

"I need their names and addresses...descriptions, anything you have on them."

"Sure, you know I'll do anything I can to help, Ron."

Jim Jernigan walked to his desk and got the register he kept the entries in. "Yeah, here's the guy on the cameo...Sam Snow, looked about eighteen. Here's the address. Anderson Street. The guy that sold me the stereo was another young guy, a Jack Blake—lives on East Lincoln."

"Thanks, Jim. I owe you one."

"When do I collect?"

I smiled and walked toward the door. "I'll dance at your next wedding."

"They ain't gonna be a next weddin'! After what I lost in the last divorce I'm callin' it quits."

I snickered and pushed open the door. This was the start of what we needed.

By now there had been 31 auto break ins—a lot for our town. Everything from old Chevys to new Town Cars. And the vics were getting peeved off bad. Another break was that I had lifted some fingerprints from the car that the stereo that Jim gave me came from. They weren't in the system.

I went back to the station and ran the names Jim had given me, and called Mrs. Jacobs on the cameo. Snow was an eighteen year old white male who had a prior on a drug charge—possession of a rolling meth lab. He had pled no contest and been given time served and three years probation. His probation, unfortunately, had ended six months ago. Brown was nowhere in our system. He had moved to the area only a few weeks before we got the first call. But the MO on the car break ins varied greatly from case to case, meaning we evidently had a number of perps involved. Also, there seemed to be about three major areas in which the incidents were taking place. Several of the missing items had showed up in dumpsters—obviously deemed unmarketable.

A gentle knock came at my office door as I was lost in thought over just what the Sam Hill was going on. "Ron," Sherry said, this is Mrs. Jacobs. She's here about the cameo."

"Sure," I said, rising and extending my hand. "Come on in, Mrs. Jacobs, have a seat."

"Please, call me Cindy," she grinned widely, and batted her eyes. "Mrs. Jacobs is my ex-mother-in-law."

The lady setting down before me was fortyish and had natural red hair. Not a bad looker, but I wasn't in the market for a woman. I raised my eyebrows and looked her in the eye.

"Okay, *Cindy*, as I told you on the phone, I picked up a cameo matching the description of the one taken from your Firebird this morning from a pawn shop here in town." I reached in my desk drawer and took the pin out, laying it on the desk in front of her.

Reflections of an Investigator

"That's it! That's my cameo!"

"How can you be sure?" I asked, narrowing my eyes a bit.

"See this little notch in the top of the stone, just over the head? That's how I can tell it's mine. When my mother gave it to me—it's an heirloom, you know—she told me about that little nick. It has a kind of darkness to it. This is an old pin."

"I see. And why did you leave it in your car, then? You know there's been a lot of break ins lately."

"I didn't leave it in the car on purpose. In fact, I didn't know what had happened to it until we found out the car had been broken into. The police scanner was taken, too, you know. I had it in my purse to show it to a friend of mine who appraises antique jewelry. It must have dropped out when I hit my brake at the red light that evening on the way home from Winchester. A squirrel ran across the road in front of me. I just can't stand the thought of killing one of the cute little things."

"I know. I try to miss animals too when they run in front of me," I said with a nod. Her story seemed reasonable. "Well, we're going to have to hang onto the cameo for evidence right now. Would you be willing to testify in court that this is your cameo?"

"Why sure, Ron. Just as long as I can get it back."

"No problem. As soon as this nightmare is over."

"Do you have any suspects?'

"I'm not at liberty to comment on that at this time," I said, rising and walking her toward the door. "I'll be in touch," I continued, shaking her hand.

The real fun was just beginning.

Chapter Seven

The newspaper wouldn't let me catch my breath. The sheer number of the break ins was enough to make any officer fidgety. Billfolds and purses were also being lifted. Side glasses and vents were being broken out of the vehicles to gain entry. I had given a statement to the media that people should be aware of the problem, not leave desirables in plain sight in their cars, and lock them every time they parked. The head of Investigations also was closing in on me to make some headway. It was time for action.

I got Scot Jackson to accompany me and called on our "old friend," Sam Snow.

When I knocked at his door, I was surprised to see him actually answer.

"Hey, Sam, remember me, Ron Cunningham?"

"Sure, Ron. How could I forget." Snow pushed open the storm door of his yellow frame house and asked us in. "What's hap'nin' dude?"

"We need you to come down to the station with us and answer a few questions for us."

"I'm not on probation any more, ya know. What do you need?"

Reflections of an Investigator

"Not here. Let's go to the station."

Snow hesitated, but apparently didn't want to look guilty. "Okay, let me get my umbrella. It's awfully cloudy, it might rain."

I watched him with hawk eyes. There was just something shifty about his actions, but all went well, and we got the suspect into the back of our car, and drove to HQ.

As soon as he was seated in the office, I got the cameo and pushed it across the desk at him. "Recognize this?" I said in a curt tone.

"Why should I?"

"Because I picked it up at Tullahoma Pawn and Loans. Jim Jernigan says you sold it to him."

Sam Snow picked up the pin and examined it closely. "I don't know. It could be the one I bought from a young lady who needed a few bucks for groceries. I got it for a little of nothing."

"Do you have proof of that?"

"What do you think I am? I'm just a guy trying to make a living. I trade on stuff."

"Don't make any plans for leaving town, Snow. We're going to get to the bottom of this, and we want you to know your name's on our list."

The next step was to check out Brown. At first attempt, he wasn't home, so we set up a stake out. As luck would have it, I was on duty at about 1:00 A. M. when he showed up, puffing on a weed.

My partner, Tom, and I exited the car and walked carefully toward him. Brown saw us and took off. Tom ran ahead of him, and I followed up. Within moments, the suspect was apprehended and was on the way to the station.

We didn't sleep that night and called in our Captain. I took Brown's prints, and told him we had a set of prints from the Mustang that the Panasonic deck was lifted from. He was visibly shaken. We took turns interrogating him. Maybe it was the marijuana, but we somehow were dogmatic enough that he knew we had him.

About 5:30 that morning, as the faint twinges of dawn's first light peeped through our windows, Jack Blake cracked. Having been promised a shot at leniency by the Captain for full cooperation with all authorities, he gave us Snow and six juveniles who were all a part of an area-wide theft ring which had been responsible for all of the break ins. Operating over the past three and a half months, the juveniles had clashed with the two adult perps, but each was aware of the balance of operations.

Reflections of an Investigator

After that, the case was a breeze. We picked up all of the juvies and Snow without incident. Some of the goods had ended up being swapped for drugs, some were at pawn shops in neighboring towns, and some were thrown into Tim's Ford Lake, ditches and trash bins, and, of course, some were never recovered. I made a statement to the newspaper, and the perps were taken to the grand jury and later convicted.

I hoped things could settle down and Tullahoma could get back to normal. Maybe not.

Chapter Eight

I thought we worked in a small southern town. Not quite Lynchburg, but certainly not New York City, or even Nashville. We surely couldn't be affected by gangs, now could we? Of course, I already knew the painful answer. I had been told they were here, but had not encountered them—until now.

One Friday evening in October, the first disturbing call came in.

"Hey, this is Gabe Dennis with Pepe's Pizza. I was making a delivery at Eastgate Apartments, and six crazy kids tried to rob me with a gun!"

"Sir, what happened next? Did they get any money from you?"

"Hell, no! I took off before they could stop me, but those idiots shot at my car and broke out the rear window! Lucky for me, I ducked!"

"Sir, please come by the station and give us a statement. We'll get someone right on this."

The dispatcher at the Communications Center who took the call dispatched a Tullahoma unit to Eastgate Apartments. But they were nowhere to be found when our officers arrived. The same night, the gang members took part in a drive-by shooting at Dossett Apartments, where members of a rival gang were thought to live. Luckily, no one was injured in the near-fiasco, although several residences and autos were damaged by the gunfire.

The next night the gang members ordered a cab to transport them to another apartment complex, where they once more attempted a robbery; this time, of the cab driver. After the cabbie foiled the robbery and was darting away in his cab, shots were fired at him as well.

Thanking his lucky stars that he was uninjured, the driver reported the incident to his dispatcher who called the Tullahoma Police Department. When Sergeant Charlie West and Officer Mitzi Rice got to the scene, they were able to arrest all six juveniles.

Upon questioning the suspects, aged from 14 to 16, we discovered that two were members of an Opelika, Alabama gang called IGD, which we were told was an acronym for "Insane Gangster Disciples." One of the gang members had placed the pizza order for the explicit purpose of luring the driver to the apartments.

The other officers and I learned that this and the robbery attempt were done as a part of the initiation process required for membership in this gruesome gang. We were informed while questioning the google-eyed locals that these out-of-state gangsters had come to Tullahoma to aid a local fledgling gang, which had been dubbed, the STPs (Small Town Players), in initiating new members and do battle with a rival gang in the area. One of the youths, who was from Tullahoma, had been living with his mother in Opelika, and had reportedly stolen a vehicle and led the others to Tennessee.

After the youths were charged, we carried the three from Alabama to juvenile detention in Murfreesboro. The three locals were sent home until ordered to report back to juvenile court with their peers. Forty charges awaited them, including armed robbery, vandalism, reckless endangerment, and destruction of property.

These youths received time in Juvenile, community service and probation, but we felt all a little safer with them off the streets for a while.

Chapter Nine

It was Wednesday, December 6th, 2000. The sun reflected sharply off my windshield and temporarily blinded me as I pulled into the parking lot at the station. I was conjuring up ideas for last minute Christmas presents as I walked in the door. It seems like the holidays were coming earlier and earlier every year.

It was 8:45 and I had shuffled through the morning formalities, talked with my Captain, Pat Holder, and had gotten my second mug of coffee when Pat stuck his head in my door. Investigator Jason Ferrell had been cruising down East Grizzard Street and noticed heavy smoke rising from a frame house. He had immediately contacted CCCC who had advised him that the Tullahoma Fire Department was already en route. Then, after the fire was put out, a preliminary search had turned up no one inside and Jason had driven on to the office. It had been only minutes now, and Jason had already been called by CCCC and informed that during a secondary search they had uncovered a body. Pat and Jason were on their way out to the scene and wanted me to know.

My promotion to Patrol Sergeant had come on 28 October 1988. After the work I had done on a number of cases for which I had received area-wide recognition, like those in the previous chapters and the one mentioned in the Epilogue of my last book, *Conspiracy, Book II, In Pursuit of Justice*, concerning the arrest and conviction of the man called James Lincoln for aggravated rape in the summer of 1992, I started working in Investigations even before I was given the title, which I had been officially granted in 1998. Because of my experience, I knew that if foul play was involved, at some point I would have a part in the investigation, but this would not be the day. I was meeting the mayor at City Hall where I'd been aiding with the Police Department's collection of food, money and toys for a special need family's Christmas.

When they arrived, Officer Mark Barrett was already at the scene. The remains of a white male, appearing to be in his late twenties, was sprawled out on his back on the living room floor, his face splattered with blood.

"How'd you find this man?" Jason asked, a bit flustered because he had left the scene of an apparent crime.

"He-he was covered with blankets. We didn't see him at first," Ian Nettles, the representative from the Tullahoma Fire Department said, scratching his head.

"What's this stuff?' the captain asked, more wanting an explanation than an answer.

"Christmas wrapping paper. Three rolls were under his shirt," another fireman said bluntly.

"Unreal," Jason said, reaching down to pull some small pieces of paper from the victim's underpants. "And these receipts and stuff?"

"If this is someone's idea of a joke, it's not one bit funny," Holder snapped.

Jason pulled at the paper sticking from the legs of the victim's scorched *Wrangler* jeans. "More wrapping paper!"

Officer Nettles dialed his phone. "We've got an arson here. Yeah. 604 East Grizzard. Also a body, but police investigators are already on the scene."

Nettles put his phone away and let out a deep sigh. "Well, we have an arson investigator coming."

The fire had been contained in the kitchen area. The EMTs arrived to collect the victim. Upon the lifting the corpse, they noticed that a radiant heater had been placed under the blankets and turned on in an effort to ignite the bedclothes and wrapping paper, in an attempt at burning the body.

Reflections of an Investigator

"Whew! Good thing the perp's plan was foiled," Jason said. "Only a little of this blanket was melted," he continued, pointing to the damaged area.

Jason looked up. Officer Brent Perry was strolling in.

"Hey Brent, you and Nettles help me get this evidence bagged."

As the victim was being prepared for removal, it became evident that there were numerous lacerations to his head and face. Jason and Brent snapped photos of everything at the scene, and forty items were tagged and listed in the evidence log. Captain Jackson meticulously shot a video, and a sketch was drawn of the room so that no stone would be left unturned. Under the victim's shirt there were what appeared to be several stab wounds to the entire upper torso.

Something else stood out as curious: the victim had what seemed to be a few light-colored hairs in his right hand. His hands were bagged, and after removing all paper from his clothing, the EMTs placed the remains in a body bag.

They then secured the crime scene with the normal yellow and black plastic ribbon and left.

Reflections of an Investigator

After they returned to the station, I asked Jason to give me an update on the evidence. I was following up leads on another case I'd been assigned to.

He told me that they were going to make an immediate effort to locate friends of the victim, who had been identified as Warren K. Norris, age 26.

Two days later, Jason received a page from a subject, and placed a call to him.

"Tom Brady?"

"Yeah?"

"This is Investigator Jason Ferrell, TPD. You were trying to get in touch with me?"

"Right. I understand you wanted to talk to me about Warren Norris?"

"That's right. What do you have for me?"

"Well, me and this other dude, Jerry Grant, we were at Warren's house for several hours the night before you guys found his body. We'd been smokin' dope and shootin' coke. I left about a quarter till four that next morning. I tried to give Jerry a ride, but he wouldn't go with me. Jerry begged Warren several times for more coke, but he wouldn't let him have any more. Warren said Jerry owed him $200 for the cocaine he already got, and that was all he was gettin'."

"So Grant was still there when you left, huh?"

"Yeah, I went on home. Jerry must have done this because he was so geeked up on that coke, and Warren wouldn't give him any more."

"What about money? Did Warren have any money that you saw that night?

"Yeah, for damn sure. He had between seven and eight hundred, at least."

I knew that there was no money found on Norris' body.

"I've got a job for you, and if you cooperate and get us what we need, you will not be facing any charges yourself on the drugs."

"Whatcha need?"

"Come to the station and we can talk about it--this afternoon at 2:00."

Chapter Ten

As I returned from lunch that day, I glanced in the glass window and noticed that Jason had someone in the interrogation room.

I was wrapping up on the case from the previous day and I was just happy that Jason was getting an early break. But it was just beginning.

"Here's what I need you to do," Jason said. "I'm going to put a body wire on you and I want you to go to Jerry Grant's home."

"Piece of cake. I'll do it."

When Brady talked with Grant and questioned him as instructed, the suspect began to get agitated, and denied killing Norris. He told Grant that even his own mother thought he had killed Norris. The two then went driving in Brady's car through the mobile home park where Grant lived.

Jason then took another other officer and me and drove to the park, where they stopped Brady and Grant and Jerry and instructed them to drive with them to the police station for questioning.

Of course Grant had no way of knowing that we could hear every word they were saying on the way back to the department.

"What should I tell them about you still being in there when I left?" Tom asked as he pulled away from the curb.

"Tell them that you took me home, man, what else?"

"Can't do that, Jerry. I'm just gonna tell the truth."

I couldn't see them, but I could just imagine the look on Grants' face, and see the proverbial smoke coming out his ears.

Jason Ferrell was still the officer on the case, so he took Grant into the room, where he agreed to a wavier of his Miranda rights. While doing the interrogation, Jason noticed that Grant had several marks on his hands and fingers that were consistent with cuts which can be sustained when a hand slips off a knife and down the blade while stabbing someone.

"How'd you get those gashes on your hands, Jerry?"

"I cut my fingers on some briars while running from the police."

"Running from the police, huh? When was that?"

"Just the other day. I'd been smokin' dope and had some on me. I didn't want to get caught with the stuff."

"How about the bruises and scratches on your face?"

"My wife got POed when I was out all night smokin' dope. You understand how that goes, don't you?"

Jerry's statement about what transpired that night concurred with Tom's until the time Tom left. I guess he must have known what Tom's story would be. After all, Tom had told him that he would be honest about it.

"When did you leave the Norris house?"

"Well, after Tom left, Warren told me he was getting ready to go to bed, so we smoked part of another joint, and then I walked down to the cab stand on North College Street but couldn't get anyone to come to the door. I walked on down to the Favorite Market on East Lincoln and called a cab from the pay phone."

"What time was that?"

"About 4:30 that morning."

Jason slowly scooted his chair back from the table and stood up. "Okay. I need your statement written out and signed. That'll be all for now. We'll be in touch."

Chapter Eleven

Other crimes took no holiday, as it always is in December. A local woman had been robbed in the middle of the night, and of course, I was elected to handle the investigation. It turned out that the suspect was from Moore County, and just a few miles from one of my old homes.

As hungry as I was to jump into the Norris murder case with all fours, I bit my tongue and took what they assigned to me. After all, it *was* Jason's case and he was doing a darn good job with it.

J. W. Blackburn had filed the report. Patty Purdy, a lady from Estill Springs, told him that she had been coming out of a grocery store when a man, whom she identified as the suspect, came up to the driver's side of her car, pulled a gun from his pocket, and hit her in the back of the head with it. The man then reportedly took a shopping bag from her car and drove off in a red Cadillac. According to the report, the bag contained several prescription drugs valued at about $200.00.

It seemed strange to me that the incident was not reported until three days after the fact.

Going on what I had, I arrested the suspect. Randall Sprague, and obtained a court date.

Reflections of an Investigator

In the meantime, I ran down leads on a purse snatcher and made another arrest. The purse, taken from a Tullahoma office, contained a considerable amount of cash, checks, credit cards, keys and prescription meds. Forged checks were showing up all over town. I was able to get this man a quick court date, and he was held without bond.

The first step for Jason was to contact the cab company and request records showing the time and place that Jerry Grant was picked up on the morning of December 6.

Jason then requested another meeting with Grant at the station at which time he agreed to a search of his home. Also, consent was obtained to have blood and hair samples taken at Harton Medical Center.

Jerry was then transported to the ER at Harton, where the samples were obtained, then accompanied to his residence, where he became extremely anxious when he was informed that our department was going to take a statement from his wife.

At Grant's residence, Jason discovered blood stains on the vinyl floor just inside the door. Blood swabs were immediately taken, and a diagram of the scene drawn on notebook paper.

In Sally Grant's statement, she said that Jerry had arrived at home before daylight and told her that he had been scratched on his face when he had gotten into a fight in Nashville. She indicated that he had just been released from jail a couple of days before that, and had no injuries at that time. She said that after he took a shower later, she saw blood running out of a cut on his head. She also stated that she and Jerry had not been in an argument.

When the cab records came, they *did* show a fare. He was picked up at the Scot Station on North Jackson at 8:30—four hours and about four blocks from where Grant stated that this had taken place. The driver reported dropping Grant off at his residence at 8:36 AM.

Jason paid Sally another visit on December 14th after learning that she had left Jerry and moved back in with her mother at a local apartment complex. He addressed the discrepancy of the time of his arrival at home. She admitted during this visit that he had actually gotten home around 8:30. She had further told Jason that when he arrived, he had on a toboggan and sweatshirt that didn't belong to him. She also stated that the cut on the top of his head was so severe that his scalp was sticking up and that when he took a shower there was an excessive amount of blood all over the shower stall and running down the drain. She explained that she had lied the first time because he was there and she knew we would have believed that he killed Norris.

Grant was arrested and charged with first-degree murder, felony murder, especially aggravated robbery, and arson of real property.

A number of us were involved in taking numerous statements from neighbors of the victim, and other parties of interest, to make our case rock-solid against Grant. The entire investigation took eleven months. I even requested that Grant take a polygraph, which was carried out at the Coffee County jail on January 10th, 2001. The evidence showed that Norris had been struck in the head with a blunt instrument and stabbed seventy-seven times.

Grant denied his guilt during the test, which "concluded that (Grant) was practicing deception when answering the relevant questions."

The evidence was insurmountable—we had him dead to rights. We also had autopsy findings from the ME's office, fingerprints, crime scene evidence, Grant's orange-handled *Tennessee Vols* pocket-knife, DNA from hair and various blood samples, tapes, and the transcripts to take to court, and some of the language wasn't pretty. The file filled an entire large black notebook.

Still he entered a plea of not guilty.

Chapter Twelve

Any place where drugs are stored becomes a target with all of the addicts in today's world, and Harton Medical Center is no exception.

A hospital employee discovered one Friday that a supply of drugs, including duramorph, versed and fentnyl was missing from a locked cart in the OB area and contacted our department. Officer Dale Stone did the report and I was assigned to the case as the investigator.

In the course of the investigation I found that an employee of a Nashville company doing contract work at Harton, who had no authority to be there, had been seen in the area from which the drugs had been taken.

After questioning several local employees, I showed up the next Monday morning and took the suspect in for questioning. Eventually I made the arrest, and we were able to recover all of the missing drugs.

During the same time frame, while we were waiting on the Grant case to go to court, about $5,000 worth of property was stolen from the Ada Ferrell Apartments between January 26th and February 2nd. In the duty of protecting and defending, there are no real guarantees, and vacations from crime, even in a city the size of Tullahoma. Mark Burnett was the officer who worked this up, and I was working on the case. But to me, it looked like an inside job.

At his trial, Grant put on his finest face. He appeared clean-shaven and neatly dressed, and his normally-shoulder-length brown hair had been cut and was properly combed.

District Attorney General Mickey Layne, who prosecuted the case, told the jurors not to let this neat young man fool them. He was 'not the same' as the suspect viewed by the police on the day Norris died. He showed them photos of the unkempt Grant a year earlier which indeed portrayed him with scraggly facial growth and lengthy hair, sporting scratches allegedly acquired during the committing of the heinous crime for which he was being tried.

Finally, three days later, the jury returned.

"Have you reached a verdict?"

"We have your honor."

The bailiff took the paper and handed it to the judge. "So say ye all?"

"So say we all."

Grant sat stoically, never blinking as the verdict was read.

"On count one, murder in the first degree, guilty; On count two, felony murder, guilty; on count three, especially aggravated robbery, guilty; on count four, arson of real property, guilty."

"Thank you, jury, you may be excused. Sentencing will be held a week from today. Bailiff, remand the prisoner and have him returned to the jail.

Chapter Thirteen

Jerry Grant was sentenced to one hundred sixty-four years with no chance of parole, and is serving his time in the State Penitentiary.

Jason really gets credit for that, and he truly did a marvelous job. But I was still handling a fair share of the investigations, and my work had not gone unnoticed.

Then, in 2001, I had been elevated to Captain of Investigations. In the years from my acceptance of the open position on the Tullahoma force on 17 August 1984, until I was promoted to Captain, I say with all humility that I had been directly or indirectly responsible for numerous indictments and convictions, for which I am very thankful. Those years now sometimes seem like a blur—they passed so swiftly. But the promotion even strengthened my resolve to be of service to Tullahoma and my desire to make this area a better place for all to live, work, and bring up their children.

Before the sun's rays had cracked the eastern horizon that Tuesday, October 10th, I received a call from C. B. Watkins, the Fire Chief.

"We need you out on East Blackwell as soon as you can get your pants on. Our men came out on a fire call about 3:00 this morning and when the fellas got the fire out and were checking for causes, they discovered a body."

"Sorry to hear it, Chief. I'll be there shortly." It almost seemed like déjà vu, and chills were creeping up my spine thinking about the Norris case.

I called Robert Burns who drove out to help me with the investigation.

When I arrived at the scene the coroner was still on hand, but the victim had already been taken away in a body bag. First thing I did after talking with Agent William Barker with the State Fire Marshall's office and getting an update was to call the DA's office and ask for the head investigator. He wasn't available, so they sent his assistant.

"Hi, have we met? I'm Ron Cunningham."

"Not sure, I handled a case down here a few years back, I believe. Ian Nettles. What do we know for sure at this point?" he asked.

I immediately remembered Nettles' name from Jason dealing with him on the Thomas case.

"Well, the victim's body has been taken to the hospital, but it's going to the State Medical Examiner's office," I told him. "According to the Fire Chief, he was found in the kitchen. That's where they say the fire was likely started. He was probably forty-nine-year-old Vic Thomas, who lived at this address, but he was pretty badly burned, so we'll have to check dental records and stuff like that to get a positive ID. We've ordered an autopsy to determine the cause of death."

"Anything else?"

"Oh, yeah, there was also the body of a dog—a Rottweiler—found in the living room. Smoke got him, they think."

"Appreciate what you're doing here," Nettles said, shuffling some forms and taking notes. "I'll file a report, but it was likely a heart attack or something. Let me know if you find out anything else."

Something just didn't seem kosher to me. The poor man had died in the kitchen, and his dog wasn't even at his side. After the investigator drove off, I decided to do a little foot work on my own, so I took Bob Burns and started a canvass of the neighborhood.

I knocked at the white asbestos-sided house on the left, and a slender elderly balding man, answered. I could smell bacon grease and it almost made me hungry.

"Sir," I said in a loud voice, "I'm Ron Cunningham with the Police Department. Did you see anything strange over at the Thomas house yesterday or last night?"

"Ya don't have to yell, I ain't deef! Jest old."

"Sorry," I backed off and smiled.

"I been out o' town the last few days, and just got back early this mornin', so I cain't hep ya none. Wish I could. I saw 'em takin' out th' body," tears were beginning to form in the old man's eyes. "He was a nice fella, as far as I knowed. Didn't talk to him all that much, but he minded his own business an' didn't give me no trouble."

"Thanks any way."

Bob and I turned and walked back to the Thomas house.

"Let's go across the alley to the other house next door," I said, as I led the way.

The front of the house was half-brick and half beige frame with a dented storm door. An attractive young teen-aged girl answered my knock.

"Can I help you?" Her voice was a bit yawn-y, so I figured the fire had kept her awake.

"Yeah, I'm Captain Ron Cunningham with the Tullahoma Police Department. I'm investigating the fire next door." By this time another young girl had come up beside her. "Did either of you young ladies see anything unusual at the Thomas house last night? Was anyone else around the house?"

"Funny you should ask," the first girl said. "By the way, I'm Linda Hill, and this is Peggy Bates, my BFF..."

"BFF? What's that?"

Both girls beamed, giggled and looked at one another. "Best Friend Forever... but anyway, Peggy spent the night with me. I saw these two guys in the yard over at Vic's yesterday afternoon. Everything seemed to be okay. Then, after Peggy got here we were camping out on the trampoline in our back yard last night, and between 10:30 and 11:00 we saw the same two guys walking down the alley. In about ten or fifteen minutes they went up on Vic's front porch. About ten minutes later, I saw Vic pull up in his van. He went into the house with the other guys and left his headlights on in his van."

"About what time was that?" I asked.

"I guess that was about 11:30 or 12:00. I remember smelling smoke and hearing some kind of beeping... I was so sleepy. Right after that we went to sleep.... probably around 12:30 or 1:00. The next thing we knew, sirens were going off and we saw the fire trucks pulling up, and the house going up in flames. That was about 3:00 this morning."

"Do you know these men?"

"Sure. They're friends of Vic's, so we didn't think anything of it."

"Uh-huh. And what are they're names?"

"One of them is Mickey Snider," Peggy volunteered. "The other guy was James Smithson."

"I'm going to need you girls to come down to the station and give me a written statement," I said.

The girls followed Bob and me back to headquarters. After taking their statements, they give me the address where Snider was staying. They didn't know where I could find Smithson. By this time the morning was half-spent.

I got on my cell phone and called Agent Barker who had gone back to his office. "Bill," I said, "I've got information that two guys were in the Thomas house right before the fire. Will you go with me? This Snider guy, that we were told was in the house last night, lives out 41 A with his aunt."

"Sure. Why not?"

We found Mickey Snider right away, and he accompanied us back to the station where he was read his rights.

I assigned Robert Burns and Jason Ferrell to question Snider while I said goodbye to my friend, Bill Barker, and went to lunch at Shannon's, one of my favorite buffets in Tullahoma.

Snider signed a waver of his rights and gave a three-page detailed written statement of his version of the events of the previous day.

In the statement he admitted that he had gone to the Thomas house the night before with James Smithson, with whom he had been all day. He said that they had all been drinking. That evening, he said, he had called Pizza Hut to order a pizza, and they had first gone to pick it up, and then went to someone else's house, and by the liquor store, where Vic Thomas had bought some *Wild Turkey*. He said that Vic wanted to go to a bar, but James didn't want to.

They then went back to Vic's where they started drinking again, and eating the pizza. He said he asked to take a shower, and Vic said he could. When he got out of the shower, James and Vic Thomas had gotten into a fight. He said that he then grabbed Thomas and that Smithson came at him with a knife and stabbed him in the back. He said Vic and James struggled for the knife and Vic got cut on the chest. He said he then took Vic's arm, and the knife dropped and he proceeded to choke him to the point of unconsciousness.

He further stated that when Thomas started coming to, Smithson told him to "get him." He said that he started to choke him again and that James jumped on him and stabbed him in the neck. He stated that Smithson then gave him the knife, and he pulled his head back by the hair and cut his throat. He stated that he went to wash his hands and James "piled stuff on top of him" and lit the fire before he came out of the bathroom. He said he took off his clothes, and threw them and his wallet into the fire before they left.

He claimed that James told him later that he had taken $24.00 in cash from Thomas before he lit the fire.

He further stated that they immediately went from there to a house on Brown Street that was under construction, where he told us we could find Smithson. He had later burned his boxer shorts as well.

Late that afternoon, Jason Ferrell and I went to the house and picked up Smithson without incident. Jason then took him into a separate room, advised him of his rights and questioned him. He denied being with Snider the previous night and seemed determined to be a problem. Since we couldn't get anything concrete out of him right then, he was taken to the Coffee County Jail in Manchester.

Chapter Fourteen

After giving Smithson a chance to sit in behind bars awhile and stew, the next afternoon we brought him back in for a 'once-over.'

This time Jason Ferrell had a plan. He and Bob Burns went in to the interrogation room together.

"Okay, Smithson, I read you your rights yesterday, any questions about that?"

"I know my damn rights."

"Good. When I'm through with you, you'll wish you'd never been born." Ferrell slammed the file in his hand onto the desk top, and leaned in toward Smithson's face.

Smithson flinched, and his eyebrows flew up.

"We've got testimony right here from three people putting you at Vic Thomas' night before last at the time the fire was started. Your buddy, Mickey, says you stabbed Vic Thomas first. Then he cut his throat and you both started the fire. He says you took $24.00 in cash off the body. We've got you both! His testimony will put you away and get the keys thrown away! Or maybe the death sentence."

"He's lying! Yeah, I was there, and got in a fight with Vic, alright, but that's not the way it went down."

Smithson was wiping the sweat from his brow, wondering who turned up the heat. Jason's eyes were drilling into his soul like an auger.

"Okay! I'll tell you what really happened. We were all just shootin' the bull, and Vic asked me if I wanted a joint. I told him since I was on probation, I better not. That damn dog of Vic's was pissing on the floor. I was drinking quite a bit and yelled at that freakin' dog. Vic told me not to yell at his dog, and came at me with a steak knife. He cut me across the chest. I grabbed his hand and wrist and pushed the knife away, towards Vic, and it cut him on the left shoulder."

Jason and Bob listened intently as Smithson continued.

"Mickey saw us fightin' and tackled Vic, and took him down. They were wrestlin' around for what seemed like forever, and I saw Mickey cut Vic's throat. Mickey got up and we were talkin' about what we were gonna do. Mickey told me we needed to get rid of all the evidence, so I piled some pillows and blankets on Vic's body and Mickey set it on fire with his lighter.

"We didn't check to see if he was still breathing. But I didn't take any money off him."

"What did you do then?"

"I left and went home. Mickey came by my house about daylight. He told me he was gonna burn his clothes since there was so much blood on 'em."

"Put that in writing for me."

Bob brought the file to me with Smithson's signed statement.

"Good job, fellas. It's up to the Grand Jury where we go from here," I said, "Take him back to the jail."

Chapter Fifteen

The age of the Internet has proven to be both a blessing and a curse. On one hand, it has given us quicker access to records and brought research to the fingertips of the average man and woman on the street.

On the other hand, it has provided predators and pedophiles countless avenues to play havoc on unsuspecting victims. Sometimes scams start by something as "innocent" as two individuals meeting on a social networking sight, or, like one case with which we were involved, an on-line game.

Some of these "games" are ominously dangerous by their very nature. One such game is called "Dungeons and Dragons," a non-traditional "wargame" which was originally designed by two young men in 1974, and was published for home use before it became available on the world-wide web. It was the original pattern for "role-playing" games and spawned the industry. Each player assumes the role of a specific character within a fantasy setting, and a "Dungeon Master" serves as the referee. Their goals are to engage in searches for treasure and knowledge. The points gained give the players power over their opponents in a series of sessions. Through the years it has gained precedence as a pop-culture phenomenon. This is primarily because the game has taken control over the minds and drives of many players to an alarming degree. In addition, now that is played on-line, it gives predators a chance to gain control over their victims.

On December 28, our Chief at the time, J. C. Ferrell, received a letter from a pastor in Pennsylvania stating that he was very concerned that a local elderly couple was being victimized by their granddaughter who was heavily involved in a role-play game on the Internet. He stated that his son had informed him early that month that he had met a young lady from Tennessee on an Internet game, later identified as Dungeons and Dragons, who planned to come to Pennsylvania. The letter further stated that she had sent his son "a couple of checks in advance." He said that he had been told that the checks were Christmas gifts to his son from the young lady's mother, and he had expected that the checks would be in the range from $10.00 to $50.00. However, when he learned that they were for $2,859.00 and $500.00, he became very alarmed. Then upon noticing that the checks, dated December 19 and 21, respectively, were 51 check numbers apart, he became more certain than ever that something was dreadfully amiss.

The young lady, Ginger Denise Silvers, age 19, was to fly to Baltimore on December 31st to meet the pastor's son, and the pastor said in the letter that he "prayed that the Tullahoma police would get to her grandparents' home before then to see if they were missing any checks."

When we went to the grandparents' residence, it was easy to ascertain that she had indeed forged the checks on her grandparents' account, and many more as well; depositing two other checks into the pastor's son's account totaling an additional $1,231.00.

Upon investigation, I learned that Miss Silvers had been living in Los Angeles prior to becoming estranged from her mother, and then moved to Detroit, where she had a boyfriend at the time. She later traveled to Nashville, where, in early December her grandparents met her and took her to their home in Tullahoma.

When we arrested Miss Silvers, she told us that she had forged 12 checks for $15,300, and burned the rest of the four checkbooks that were missing. However, we found that this was untrue, because other checks kept showing up. Her grandparents were devastated.

With the assistance of a fraud and theft specialist at AEDC Federal Credit Union, which stopped payment on all outstanding checks, we were able to keep any of the forged checks from clearing the bank.

She had set up a bank account in Hawaii, where she and the pastor's son planned on moving after their meeting in Baltimore.

The largest check was earmarked for a deposit on "a house" for the girl and the pastor's son, who claimed he was "shocked to learn what happened," and cooperated with the investigation.

Miss Silvers waived her right to a preliminary hearing and was bound over to the Grand Jury and subsequently convicted on charges of Forgery and Theft.

As I told the reporter with the *Tullahoma News*, "Only holiday delays and a timely notice from the pastor saved them from potential liability for thousands of dollars more than they had in their life savings."

Chapter Sixteen

A few days after the Thomas murder and arson I received a call from the State Medical Examiner's office in Nashville saying that he had obtained dental records, and done an autopsy which proved that the body was indeed that of Vic Thomas. No surprise there, but we needed the report for the records. We had obtained search permits and gone over the scene with a fine-toothed comb.

The case was carried over to the Grand Jury, and a court date set. In the meantime, the suspects were working with their public defender to cop a plea.

Since Smithson was on probation at the time of the incident, he was walking a dangerous plank.

But, as I said in the beginning of this book, a law enforcement officer never knows what a day will bring. There is never a dull moment for an investigator.

One Monday we got a call at the Department that the body of a mixed-race male baby, appearing to be about two weeks of age, had been found by a maintenance worker in a dumpster at Continental Apartments at approximately 9:42 that morning. Mizi Rice took the call and requested that a team go to the location to do the investigation and secure the crime scene. I went, of course, along with Officers Tildon Stubblefield and Johnny Gore. We also phoned District Attorney Mickey Layne, who called for a medical examiner. The body was transported to Harton Regional Medical Center, and examined by Dr. Charles Harlan, who then took the baby to his headquarters at the State Medical Examiner's Office in Nashville.

When we questioned the worker, who it seemed was frequently rummaged the dumpsters, and on this occasion, we learned that the infant had been tidily wrapped in two blankets with a small teddy bear, and placed in an Emerson VCR box.

Believing that the carton may contain a VCR, the maintenance worker opened it—something the perpetrator evidently had not expected. After removing the tape from the box, the infant's head and shoulders were exposed.

The exact time of death had not been determined, but the state of decomposition indicated that death had occurred several days prior. The garbage truck, I was told, had picked up the contents of the dumpster only minutes before the body was discovered. It appeared to me that someone local had been responsible for discarding the body in this particular location.

Reflections of an Investigator

With this case and others crying for a solution, illegal drug trafficking had not been halted, but we were making fantastic headway in the battle.

For five months we had been planning a huge drug sting along with support from officers in three counties: Coffee, of course, Franklin, and Moore, all of which were part of the capital metropolitan area. In April we wrapped up by far the largest drug roundup that had taken place in the city's history.

We had set up sixty-five undercover officers from eleven different agencies which became involved in buying controlled and illegal drugs, videotaping the transactions in Tullahoma. Some participating officers were from as far away as LaVergne, and some were members of the Interstate Police Force.

As a result of this bust, eighty-five indictments were handed down from the Coffee County Grand Jury. Several were repeat offenders, and some whom we would label as career offenders, but a few were first-timers. Suspects were charged with both Class B and C felonies. Some were sent away for lengthy sentences.

D.A. Layne was quick to praise the sting as a smashing success. "The operation has been run professionally, and it has been thoroughly documented," he told *The Tullahoma News*. "It was on a larger scale than any in the last eight years and ran so smoothly that those who participated can be proud of what they accomplished."

Although it was not my division's project, per se, I was glad to have been a part of it, and a part of Chief Ferrell's excellent team.

Chapter Seventeen

It was a simmering June afternoon. All of the things I would like to do that weekend were rolling around in my mind. About 3:30 I heard the buzzer on the front office door and knew that someone was on their way in. Two Coffee County deputies, Sherrill and Elliott, soon knocked on my door, followed by Tullahoma Officer, Charlie West.

"Hey fellas, come on in," I said rising and reaching out to shake their hands.

"Hey, Ron, Sheriff Graves told us to go out to 210 Black Gum Street and try to find a guy named Gerald Nesmith. He jumped bond," Deputy Sherrill said, hardly waiting for me to reach his hand.

"Yeah, Ron, I came in because earlier today Sergeant Higginbotham told me that Nesmith was supposed to be at Harold Buchannan's house, which I know is at 205 Black Gum. I think that's where you want to go, 205, not 210."

"Okay, I'll get a couple more of my men and we'll go check this guy out," I said.

I asked Detectives Johnny Gore and Bob Burns to come with us, and we all loaded up and headed for 205 Black Gum Street. The two deputies pulled in behind us and ambled up to the door while we waited in my SUV.

A white male of medium build answered, identifying himself as Gerald John. I wondered if it was really Gerald Nesmith. I could see Sherrill pealing back layers of paper, then placing John under arrest. It turned out that he was also a wanted man with open warrants in Tennessee.

Following placing John into their patrol car, the deputies asked Gore and Burns to accompany them back to the door. This time they were greeted by a twenty-something female subject who gave them permission to search the house.

West and I stayed outside and kept a watch on the premises. In a few minutes the deputies came back out and informed us that the female had told them that Nesmith was upstairs.

At that point we all walked to the rear of the home where a stairway ascended to a second floor apartment, which was separated from the main floor. We made our way up, and the apartment door was standing wide open, so we eased our way in. A television was blaring, but there was no occupant to be found.

We all went back down to the street, and the deputies knocked at the house next door. West,

Gore, Burns and I were standing by the edge of the street, about two feet off of the pavement toward the Buchannan house.

"Here comes Harold!" Burns yelled.

West and I looked up in unison and observed Buchannan storming toward them from the direction on Malibu Drive.

"You don't have due process!" Buchanan spurted at me.

"Probable cause," West retorted, "I think you mean probable cause."

"Get the hell off my damn property!" Buchannan snorted.

It seemed obvious to us that we were on the street right of way, but apparently he didn't see it that way.

Buchannan wasn't about to give up his tirade. His eyes were glaring at both of us. But it was me he came after! He bounded closer to me and squared off, readying himself for a fight. Then, he made a swing at my face.

I could vaguely hear Charlie calling for a marked unit.

I moved my head backward only slightly, but his fist nicked my glasses and they plunged to the ground. His long, greasy hair flipped from side to side as he pivoted about bolting his fists around like a prizefighter getting ready for the one-two KO. I reached over his extended arm and grabbed a handful of that greasy hair, jerking him toward me. Then with my right knee I caught him in his beer belly. I pulled his head over my raised knee with lightening speed, causing him to loose his balance, plunging him to the ground. I then placed my knee on his chest, dropping my head to meet his face in a close-up-and-personal way that I would never have desired had circumstances not mandated it.

"Put your hands behind you!" I commanded gruffly.

Bob Burns was upon him in a New York minute, clamping the cuffs on his wriggling wrists.

I reached down and retrieved my glasses, wiped the clotting blood from the scratch on my nose with my handkerchief, and scrambled to my feet.

Neighbors were getting the eyes full, which would later be helpful for statements to back up the cause for our arrest.

The other officers had now arrived, and Rana Pawlowski put Buchannan into her patrol car. I hopped in with Rana and Conroy to transport the prisoner to the jail. But the taunting and raving continued, with threats of what he would do when he got out of the car.

We pulled into the Sally Port, and removed the suspect. Silence was upon his lips until we locked him in the bull pen. At least now he couldn't carry out his devilish threats.

27-year-old Buchannan was charged with assault on a police officer and resisting arrest. His bond was set at $7,500.00.

A short time later, we received information that Gerald Nesmith was at a bar on South Jackson. Gore and Burns took him into custody there and transported him to the Sheriff's Department without further incident.

Chapter Eighteen

We had just celebrated our country's independence the day before with a great air show and spectacular fireworks that evening. One of the local Kiwanis Clubs always has 'Fly the Flag' that day, and the merchants participate in groves. It had been 229 years of freedom from England. I have always taken pride in being an American. It was July 5, 2005—less than a month had passed, however, since our arrest of Harold Buchannan.

The phone at headquarters rang and Captain Scott Jackson answered. It was Deputy Mike Rainy from my old stomping grounds in Moore County.

"I need you fellas to assist us in recovering a truck that a guy here loaned to a relative there in Tullahoma."

"Sure, anything to help, Mike," Jackson said.

"Hey, West," Jackson motioned after getting the details. "I need your help. Here's the scoop on this truck. I need some help. The guy who owns it is coming by."

"Sure, Captain," Charlie West said, "Our officers will go out with the complainant while either you or the owner picks up the truck, but we can't make an arrest 'cause there's no warrant on file."

About 1:10 P.M., Kent Krueger, the complainant, arrived at the station. It turned out that the truck had been loaned to his grandson, Freddy Krueger, and he had refused to relinquish it. He told Charlie that the truck was parked at 205 Black Gum Street. *Oh, no*, I thought, my head dropping to my chest, *the Buchannan house!*

I was in earshot of all of this and the grandson's name gave me shivers when I heard it. I could picture Krueger with scars all over his face and a black hat coming after us. And then there was the even more realistic and sickening thought of dealing with Buchannan again, who was out on bond. Maybe I was caught in the Nightmare on Black Gum Street! It all seemed a bit surreal.

Charlie told Kent that he would drive down with him, but that *he* would have to go to the door and ask for Freddy. Then, the new nightmare started. Charlie looked straight at me and asked me to go along. I guess he thought I was a glutton for punishment.

When Charlie parked his cruiser next door, he and I got out. Sure enough, there was the truck in question parked on the shoulder in front of us. We walked up next to the truck while Kent went to the door. Buchannan met Kent. His look wasn't that of a fan.

"What the hell do *you* want?"

"I need to talk to my grandson, Freddy."

"Freddy ain't here."

"I need to get my truck. Where are the keys?"

"I don't know *where* the keys are!"

Buchannan's head swiveled, his gaze met ours, and his finger pointing at us looked like the muzzle of a gun.

"I got no problem with you wantin' your truck, but what are those mother****ers doin' here?"

Buchannan's voice was highly elevated. Kent Krueger made his way back to us; then West called Communications on his cell and asked them to locate a locksmith for us.

"Kent, while we're waiting for the locksmith, why don't you look through the truck and see if the keys might be in there somewhere?" Charlie said.

"I'm gonna get you, a**hole! You're dead meat!" His arms went into place as a sniper with an assault rifle, "Click! You're dead, man!"

I kept a straight face, refusing to give him pleasure.

"It's comin', it's comin'!" Buchannan taunted.

I continued to pretend I wasn't in the middle of my second nightmare on Black Gum Street. But he kept up his act, calling us those god-awful names, raising his arms and making a shooting sound with his tongue.

Kent soon found his keys in the truck and Charlie told him to start it and get away from there in a hurry.

West and I then drove away with Buchannan hurling threats in our rear view.

Chapter Nineteen

Early one morning, not long after that, I had just come in, checked my email, and settled down at my desk with a nice hot cup of brew when I got a call from a Shelbyville Police Detective with whom I had had dealings.

"Hey Ron, Chris Szaroleta."

"Hey, man, what's happening?"

"I've been investigating a $4,000 burglary at a rent-to-own store here."

"Hmm. How can I help?"

"I've already picked up a suspect, a Casey Guy Pettis, 23, and he's still in custody."

I was nodding. Pettis was no stranger to me. First, he was a native of my old stomping grounds in Moore County, and secondly, he was also a person of interest in some local petty burglaries in Tullahoma.

"Uh, huh. I know him, but why do I feel this has more to it?"

"Pettis implicated an 18 year old from Tullahoma. Nate Redden."

Again my head was wagging blithely.

"Now you've got my attention. Both of these guys are suspects in a case here—we just didn't have enough to go after Redden—it's all circumstantial."

Maybe this can help me pull our case together, too, I thought.

"I'll pick him up," I told Szaroleta, unless you want to meet me over here and go with me to get Redden."

"That's kinda what I had in mind," Chris said. "I'll see you in about thirty minutes."

My eyes widened and I looked at my watch. "Okay, I've got a meeting with the Chief. Could you make it an hour?"

"Sure. See you about 8:45 to 9:00."

I gulped down my java and knocked on the Chief's door. I told him about the development and how I thought it might tie in with our case, covered his agenda, and met Szaroleta at five till nine.

I had the address ready and we hit the street. It was only a short drive from our office, out of town. When we rang the doorbell, we saw a curtain move ever so slightly. A heavy-set fortyish lady with stringy black hair came to the door.

"Ma'am," I said slowly, "we're looking for Nate. Is he around?"

"Who are you guys?" she said, wrinkling her forehead. "Whatcha want with Nate?"

"I'm an investigator with the Tullahoma Police Department, ma'am, are you his mother?"

"Is Nate in some sort of trouble?"

"Well, ma'am, we just need to ask him some questions. Are you his mother?" I said.

"Yeah, that's me. Nate stays up about all night, I'm afraid he's not outta bed yet."

"Well, ma'am, we need you to get him up."

The mother released her firm hold on the old wooden door, turned and yelled. "I guess I'm gonna have to go in there," she said shortly. "You know how these kids are nowadays."

We were still standing on the stoop, and Szaroleta was holding the storm door open. From the looks of the inside of the house I surmised that she was ashamed to ask us in.

It was a full fifteen minutes before she brought the youth in, rubbing his eyes, and reaching for a cigarette.

"Nate," I started, "I'm Ron Cunningham, Tullahoma Police Department. We need you to come down to the station and answer some questions for us."

"Questions? What about?"

"Well, we really need to go to the station," I answered. "It's not something I want to talk about here."

Nate looked down. It was hard to see the expression on his face, but it seemed I could almost hear his brain trying to get into gear. If he ran, he would be admitting guilt—in front of his mother. If he said too much he might make her think he was trying to get out of cooperating with the law.

"Okay," he finally said with a slight cough. Then turning to his mother, "Be back in a little bit. If Joe calls tell him I'm still planning on going with him to the lake fishing."

When we got to the station, we put him in a room and advised him of his rights. He said he had nothing to hide. Chris Szaroleta and I both went in to question him.

"Where were you on the night of September 18th between the hours of 11:00 and 12:30?" Szaroleta asked.

"Whadaya think I am? I don't keep up with where I am ever minute. I'm usually home that time of night."

"That wasn't that long ago. It was a Saturday night, and you know what I'm talking about. Do you know a Casey Pettis?"

There was a visible shift in Nate Redden's eyes. Then there was a pregnant pause before he answered.

"Well, yeah! We hang some together. What's he got to do with this?"

"Give it up, Nate," Szaroleta said, hitting the desk with his fist close to his face. "We've got you. Pettis already gave you up. You were with him in the break in and burglary of Bestway Rent-To-Own in Shelbyville that night."

Redden was reticent, his eyes almost seemed glazed over.

"We've also got information that puts you with him in four burglaries here in Tullahoma," I said.

"That's a damn lie!" Nate said, jumping almost straight up. "I wasn't with him on any of those! He did those by himself!"

I pushed him down on both shoulders, and his head flew back. "Nate, calm down," I said softly. "If you can prove that we can request leniency on you."

"Damn straight, I can. Casey called me before he broke in the service station on Jackson and wanted me to go with him. I told him nothin' doin'. After the job over in Shelb'v'll, I wasn't gettin' involved anymore. I went and helped him on a dare. I shouldn't 'ave done it."

With information given us by Nate, Shelbyville Detectives Chris Szaroleta, Pat Mathis and Tony Collins, Tullahoma Detective Tilden Stubblefield and I, all of whom had done work on these cases, were able to recover all of the jewelry from the Bestway burglary. One piece was brought in from Huntsville, Alabama, and another from Elkhart, Indiana. In addition to the Shelbyville incident, Pettis was charged on four burglaries in Tullahoma. Redden was charged with only one burglary and petty theft.

In the meanwhile, Smithson and Snider of the Vick Thomas case were facing charges of first degree murder, aggravated arson, and one count of killing an animal. Smithson pled guilty to second degree murder and aggravated arson only, and received a sentence of twenty years.

Snider pled to voluntary manslaughter, aka "man one," with all other charges dismissed. He was sentenced to sixteen years.

The case of the infant in the VCR box, however, was never solved. It's a shame, but many cases go unsolved every year around the globe.

Chapter Twenty

The seasons were fleeting so swiftly that I hardly knew where the time was going. The frigid winter faded to the crisp newness of spring, and the smoldering heat of summer gave in to the brightly-painted blanket of autumn leaves. It seemed that no sooner than a year started, the winter holidays were upon us again.

That year, as always, had brought some mysterious cases our way that you wouldn't expect in our area. One strange occurrence that I can recall was four sticks of dynamite which had been found behind the office of a local attorney in a small cooler. Cathy Grady Conley had found about everything from stolen bicycles to an unopened six-pack of beer in that alley, but this one was a bit on the scary side.

I checked the evidence out thoroughly, and there were no other items present from which a bomb might have been made, which had been my first concern. Not even any blasting caps or fuses. Once I had cleared any thought of the dynamite exploding accidentally, I had taken it and placed a safe distance away from City Hall. Fire Chief Watkins had assigned three units on standby.

We had explosives experts Rick Leonard and Enoch Lankford take the dynamite to the firing range and detonate it. It left a ghastly hole three feet deep. This is our standard practice for disposal of explosives taken by the department. But the presence at Cathy's office was still a mystery.

Our family was making a regular event out of renting a cabin on the Lake at Tim's Ford as a means of getting away from it all during the holidays. It was wonderful pushing my job from my mind for a few pleasant days, even during those rare times when we got a bit of snow during the Christmas break.

For months before our getaway that December, an inundation of complaints against a local bio energy company had reached a high crescendo. The case had fallen squarely upon my shoulders.

The company, which we shall call Hackberry Energy, owned by Bonnie and Hal Beecham, had been widely accused of scamming the public.

One of the many services of the business was providing wood pellets for heating of homes. I had gotten notified of over seventy complaints by consumers that their orders where not being filled, and their requests for refunds were being ignored.

Orders had been placed on their web site, by email, and over the phone during an eight month period by 910 customers for at least $55,000 worth of the goods and services. Of the 364 customers for pellets, 40% were reported as not being delivered. As investigator on the case, I handled communications with the Beechams in an attempt to resolve the dispute.

After considerable efforts and correspondence, in mid December I had received a lengthy letter from the Beechams telling me that the pellet business, in which the complaints were regarding, was but a small part of their company, and went on to elaborate on the vast nature of their commerce.

They further explained that in an effort to find the finest product available for this tiny segment of their business they had searched for the lowest possible prices to be able to fill the orders, and attempted to explain how slowly they had been able to receive the money and fill the orders, then stated that during this extensive process the cost of wood pellets had escalated and they were unable to deliver them as promised. This had proven too much for their small (now they are small) company. They explained that the situation had reached the point of their receiving death threats.

The letter went on to say that they were "working toward refunding all pellet orders left on record." They explained that they would have to do this by check as funds permitted, as PayPal, by which much of the payments were made, would not handle refunds after 60 days. Because of the way credit card reverses were made, according to the letter, there was a danger of duplication of charge backs.

They stated emphatically that they were no longer selling wood of any type for home delivery.

I had done all I could and finally turned the case over to Consumer Affairs and the office of the Tennessee State Attorney General.

On January 8th our efforts for the consumers was rewarded. Attorney General Robert E. Cooper filed a civil suit against the company for violation of the state's Consumer Protection Act.

After the suit, Hackwood Energy attempted to file for bankruptcy, but the request was denied by the United States Trustee Office in Chattanooga, due to "Their past history and continued history of scamming the public."

Chapter Twenty-one

I couldn't have been surprised when I found out the next morning that on evening of Thursday, February 1st, 2006, there had been a fight in the alley behind the Last Stop Bar on Warren Street and someone had been badly injured. That place had been a spot of constant contention for over a year, while I had had my head in the Vic Thomas murder case, the Hackwood Energy scandal, and scores of minor offences.

Verbal arguments, a stolen car, then a possible robbery, a stolen wallet inside the bar, a stolen auto tag, a couple of other assaults, vandalism, tires slashed, a for-sure robbery and attempted kidnapping, had happened there, just to name a few.

The call had come in at 9:06 PM. I had gone off duty at 5:00. The dispatcher, Talley, immediately assigned it to Officer Tyrone Brazier, who was on patrol in the area.

Upon arriving at the bar at 9:08 PM, Tyrone saw a white male, later identified as Teddy Gauge, wearing a long-sleeved orange shirt, denim jeans and white tennis shoes, lying on a concrete pad in the rear of the building. He noticed that Gauge appeared to be semi-conscious, and had what looked to be a large contusion on the back of his head. Beside Gauge was a stack of logs. One log had fresh blood on the end of it.

911 had been called, and Coffee County EMS arrived shortly and transferred Gauge to Harton Regional Medical Center.

He first spoke with the caller, a guy named Rick, and in depth with Jade Brown, the owner and manager of the bar.

"What exactly happened here, Brown?" Brazier asked.

"Well, about 9:00 Teddy Gauge and another guy came in here through the back door. He knew he was banned from this place. The guy was always gettin' into an argument with somebody.

"This other guy who was already here, that he couldn't get along with, tried to punch Teddy and Teddy ducked and he missed.

"I don't know what happened after that. I heard raised voices outside and one of the other customers told me there was a fight goin' on in the alley. That's when I went to the door and saw him layin' out there and we called you guys."

"Who was the guy that tried to punch Gauge?"

"Charlie Brennon."

"And who told you about the fight?"

"Jimmy Scruggs. They're both still here."

"Okay, you guys, don't anybody leave. I'm going to need to talk to all of ya'll."

In his statement to Tyrone Brazier, Charlie Brennon admitted that he and Gauge had recently gotten into a fight, but denied trying to punch him that night. He said that in the previous argument he had gotten a cut on his forehead.

Scruggs said that he was in the bar the entire time. He stated that he had heard someone yelling outside, and that when he looked out, Gauge was lying on the ground.

At 9:25, Tyrone took the log into evidence and then drove to the station, informing the witnesses that they were all subject to call.

Chapter Twenty-two

I returned the next day and waded through the evidence on the Gauge assault. The victim was received in critical condition at Harton and had been airlifted to Nashville. His location was not yet being released for obvious reasons. He remained in the ICU there. His attacker was still at large and unidentified.

This whole case, which was already baffling, was about to get even more complex. The evidence was examined, the log checked for prints, and the blood sent to the lab. It was conclusively proven to match the victim.

I made a number of calls and contacts, and had several people to see.

By February 6th I had sufficient evidence and made arrests of both Brennon and Scruggs for questioning, reading them their rights.

At the station I took separate handwritten statements from them after letting them know I was not playing around, and that anything they did to cooperate could help their cases.

Brennon admitted that he, his mother, and his girlfriend were at the Last Stop Bar on the night of the assault. He stated that he was doing karaoke, and that at around 9:00 Teddy Gauge and a guy named Chip Simpson came in.

He now admitted going after Gauge and trying to hit him due to the fact that several weeks prior Gauge had 'hit him over the head with a 2X4.' He stated that he had grabbed Gauge's coat sleeve, making a swing at him, at which time Gauge had jerked away. He stated that at that time someone separated the two, and he went back to where they were doing karaoke.

"The police came in," Brennon said, "and I never did go outside. Later, I heard there was a fight out back."

In Scruggs' statement he said that when Teddy and Chip came in, Charlie was sitting in the corner.

"I saw him and grabbed his arm. He jerked away from me and went for Teddy. Teddy fell and his glasses got knocked off."

"Did Charlie actually hit him?"

"I don't know if Charlie actually hit him or not, but he did swing at him. I got Charlie back on the way up against the wall, and he pulled a knife."

"What did you do then?"

"I hollered, 'Charlie's got a knife!' and Charlie gave the knife to me."

I nodded and Scruggs continued.

"I started toward the back door and I heard someone say. 'No, Landon, no!'"

"Landon who?" I knew who he meant, because I had him on my contact list. I had found out that he was in the bar that night and told Jade Brown that I needed to talk to him.

"Landon Criswell. He's this part Indian dude from Florida."

"Go on, what happened then?"

"That's when I saw Landon coming back in the bar, and I went out in the back and saw Teddy, just layin' there on the concrete. I tried to make Teddy as comfortable as possible. Then the cops came and the ambulance and took Teddy."

I then went to the Last Stop bar and obtained a statement from Jade Brown. I gave him the gist of what I already knew and asked for a comprehensive truthful statement, indicating that anything else could cause charges to be made against him.

Brown was cordial, but I felt the tension hanging in the stale air of his bar so heavy that you could cut it with a case knife.

His statement, which was considerably altered from the one he had given on the night of the incident, agreed in principle with what Brennon had told me. He said that Brennon had knocked off Gauge's glasses, and then the sparks began to fly between them. He stated that Landon had said that he would get Teddy, and someone shouted, "Charlie has a knife."

Obviously Scruggs, I thought. Then he told me that the knife had been given to Jimmy Scruggs.

Right on target, I thought.

He said that Chip Simpson was trying to help Teddy when he went out.

"Chip told me Teddy was not responding, so I went in and told Rick to call 911."

"What did Landon do then?" I asked.

"I couldn't believe it. He came back in here and watched the game on TV!"

"Have you talked to him since?" I asked.

"Well, he called here the other day and talked to a girl that was working here."

"Do you know what he said?"

"She told me the only thing he said was, "How's Teddy doin'?"

"What did she say?"

"I told her to tell Landon he was doin' better and that you were lookin' for him."

I nodded, and left, a slight smile on my lips.

A statement was also obtained from Chip Simpson, who also implicated Criswell. Chip told me basically the same thing that Charlie and Jack had about the incident.

That day I arrested Landon Criswell and advised him of his rights. He refused to talk to me and asked for his attorney.

He called a local lawyer, whom I know well, who came to the police station. Criswell spoke to the attorney, who related his version of the incident. The attorney then wrote up his client's lengthy statement, admitting his involvement, but alleging self-defense, and obtained the signature.

Brennon and Scruggs were released on bond pending showing up for Criswell's trial.

Chapter Twenty-three

Landon Criswell, alias Grady Showls, it turned out, had an impressive rap sheet—both from Tennessee and Florida. That is if you want to impress the bad guys. Everything from worthless checks to driving on a revoked license, to narcotics violations.

After the first statement from Scruggs, he voluntarily gave me another one—one about a separate incident which he said took place four days later. He stated that on Monday evening, February 5th, he was back in the Last Stop Bar with a young man named Jason Sorrels. As he was walking toward the door to leave, somebody hit him in the face with a bottle. He fell to his knees in anguish, and somebody started kicking him. Then someone else got on his back. He stated that he managed to get up, and saw several people around him. While still dazed from getting bashed with the bottle, Jade Brown, he stated, pulled a gun, aimed it at his head, and told him he had better leave. Just then, according to Scruggs, a police officer walked in and Jade put the gun away.

By then Jason was out in the back. The officer asked Scruggs if he was alright, and he told him, 'yes,' and left.

Reflections of an Investigator

This was about the last straw for me. I couldn't likely prove any of what Scruggs said, but there was something I could do. As I said earlier, the Last Stop Bar was a constant festering sore in the eyes of our department.

The next day I filed a request with the Beer Board Secretary, Rosemary Womack, as outlined in Tullahoma Municipal Code – Title 8, Chapter 3, to set a date for a formal hearing on a grievance against the Last Stop Bar. I enclosed a complete report of the Gauge assault incident and a list of complaints over the past 14 months. This added to the fact that they had already had a first offence penalty of $1000.00 fine and 1 year probation levied against them on September 12th of 2005.

I obtained a release for medical information on February 12th, signed by the wife of the victim, and subpoenaed the records from both hospitals, which were made a part of the case against Criswell.

At their monthly meeting on February 28th, the Board heard the complaint against the Last Stop Bar, and set a hearing date.

At the hearing the board voted to shut down the establishment. Now the sore could heal.

Landon Criswell was charged with aggravated assault, with a secondary charge of violation of probation, was bound over to the Grand Jury, and went to trial on September 19th, 2007. He was found guilty and sentenced to three years in the Federal Penitentiary. After serving 11 months and 29 days, he was placed on probation for the balance of his sentence.

Chapter Twenty-four

The limited glow of my porch light reflected like candlelight on sequins off the frost which lay heavy on my yard that Wednesday morning, November 21st, 2007. I gazed out my window at that mystical scene while gulping down the last of my coffee before heading for the office. It was kind of good not to have to concern myself with how manicured the lawn was for another winter.

My wolf pup, Beowulf, jumped up on the fence and howled goodbye while the crescent moon caressed the horizon as I backed out the drive.

We had just gotten through the morning rituals at headquarters when a call came in from a frantic 13-year old boy at D.W. Wilson Recreation Center stating excitedly that a man had just made an attempted sexual assault on him at that location.

Sergeant Jason Ferrell had Harry Conway, who was catching an early lunch, take the call, as it was squarely in his line of duty.

A pre-bid process was taking place on renovation of the building, and the suspect was at the rec center to make an evaluation and come up with a bid to do the required repairs.

According to the victim and the witness, they had been playing basketball for some time in the gym during which time a man had been eyeing them. The unidentified subject had then motioned the witness to come to where he was standing. The witness stated that he had refused, and called the victim out.

Later, the two reported, the victim walked up to the subject in the hallway near the vending machines and asked him if he had played basketball, and how old he was at the time. The man reportedly had told the victim that he had indeed played on a basketball team at his age. The subject, the victim said, had then asked him if he knew what a "blow-job" was.

Shaken, the victim then asked the subject to repeat the question. After there was no doubt as to what had been said, the boy asked the man if he wanted a "blow job."

Attempting to remain calm, the youth then ran out of the building as fast as his legs would carry him. He told Jason that he had been fearful of sexual assault.

When Conway arrived at the center the subject was already gone. Surveillance videos were obtained — the second thing we had going for us. The videos showed the man, described as having an orange shirt and khaki pants, in the gym area, going into the rest room, and then making contact with the youth in the hallway as alleged. But there was no audio on the video to prove what was said.

After carefully examining the videos and running the picture of the man against state records, the subject was identified as 40-year old Lawrenceville native, Jeffrey Randall, a sub contractor who had been there to bid on the job. A warrant was obtained and the suspect was later taken into custody at his home—I will get back to this later. But he wasn't admitting to anything. Maybe this wasn't going to be a slam-dunk after all.

Chapter Twenty-five

It was the bone-chilling morning of Friday, December 28th following the Criswell trial and the Randall arrest. I had the cheery times which I had enjoyed with my wife and girls over the Christmas holidays flooding my mind as I drove to the station in my SUV. My toe tapped to the Martina McBride song ringing on the radio as I waited for it to end before cutting off my engine and going inside.

But as I walked in the door of my office, it was a different beat that I would face. The smile on my face was about to fade with the proverbial return of reality. The phone was already loudly vibrating on the hook. It was the principal of the Tullahoma High School, asking me to send an officer out and examine some delineated graffiti on a garage bay door and a new trailer that the city had recently purchased for the high school.

I sent Jason Kennedy, one of my promising young investigators, to check it out. But this, it turned out, was to be barely the tip of the ice burg. The fanciful letters, "MK" began showing up everywhere over the next few days. Several locations on Atlantic Street were chosen, and the viaduct on Carroll Street—including the old vacant Post Office building, and at Arnold's Furniture Warehouse. Then the mysterious letters appeared on a storage building at the Coffee County Senior Citizen's Center on North Collins Street, on a brick building on Highway 130, aa well as on several trash bins scattered about town. This invisible perpetrator had our heads spinning.

Thousands of dollars in damage had been done, and we had to know who was taunting us like this.

We put a plea in the *Tullahoma News* on Friday, January 11th, 2008. We also got a complaint about vandalized headstones in a local cemetery on January 26th.

But the nagging graffiti case drug on until the end of March, when things began to take a hopeful turn.

The first break I got seemed that it might put an end to the whole sordid affair. On March 20th I received another call from the high school, drove out to pick up a sixteen-year-old juvenile whom we shall call Donnie Northcutt, and took him to headquarters for questioning.

Donnie seemed like a nice boy just a bit out of his territory. He admitted to doing the current graffiti at the school and gave me a handwritten statement. He said that he had drawn M.K. on the boy's restroom wall next to the band room at the high school about two weeks before. Then he admittedly had inscribed the same letters on the 'dry race board' in one of the classrooms.

"Are you the one who's been doing all this?" I asked, though by this time knowing the answer in my heart of hearts.

"Na, I just saw it all over town, and it looked so k-o-o-l that I started practicing it till I got it. Here, I'll show you."

Donnie sketched the letters on the yellow pad on which he had written his statement and turned it around so I could see it. I nodded.

"Do you know what it means?"

"Yeah, Mass Karnage. My manager, Mack Bates, says it means Mass Karnage. I work at Wendy's. When I was at work about three weeks ago I drew M.K. on the board there and talked to Mack. He told me that's what it means. He said, 'that's someone else's tag, you don't need to be drawing it.' Now he thinks me and a friend of mine are doing this all over town. But we ain't"

"I think I can make it easy on you if you'll help us in catching the real perpetrator or perpetrators. Are you game?"

"Sure, why not? What do you want me to do?"

Two examples of the MK graffiti

Chapter Twenty-six

On March 17th Jeffrey Randall was indicted on the charge of solicitation of statutory rape. He pled not guilty and demanded a jury trial.

I contacted Donnie Northcutt's parents who reluctantly signed an order allowing their son to cooperate in the investigation in any way needed, even to utilizing audio and video equipment on his person anywhere in the county if needed.

At 2:45 P.M. on Sunday, March 30th, Officer Robert Weaver and his partner, Officer Jason Brockman, responded to a Suspicious Persons call and drove to the CSX railroad viaduct on North Atlantic Street. Upon arriving at the scene, Robert observed a car parked under the viaduct, and two young white male subjects hanging out near some parked train cars.

"Hello there!" His masculine voice echoed off the trestle. "I'm Officer Weaver with the TPD. How are you gentlemen doing today?"

The young males nodded. "Fine," one muttered.

"Which one of you owns this vehicle?"

"Me," the older boy said. The other was obviously a young juvenile, but Weaver was appealing to his pride.

"There's been a lot of vandalism in this area, and nobody needs to be here just parked. I need to see your driver's license and registration on the car, please."

"Sure, we ain't got nothin' to hide."

After checking out the paperwork and asking the name of the other boy, Weaver continued. "Mr. McCall, You said you didn't have anything to hide. May I have permission to search your car?"

The two young men looked at each other, and McCall nodded.

"There's two or three spray cans under the front seat from my friend here taggin' trees for his dad."

A search of the car turned up two cans of spray paint—one black and one orange—under the passenger's side.

"Look at this," Brockman yelled back at Weaver, "there's fresh spray paint on this train!"

"Shoot! It's wet as water!" Weaver said as his finger pulled away from the evidence.

"Which one of you did this?" Weaver asked.

The eyes of the youth widened and both shook their heads."Not me!" they said in overlapping intonation.

"Uh-huh. Mr. Nobody did this!" Brockman said, pursing his lips and wagging his head at a snail's pace.

Weaver placed both suspects under arrest, read them their rights, and then radioed Officer George Blassingame who transported the pair to headquarters.

Once they were at the station, Weaver called Harry Conway, who came in and aided Weaver in questioning the suspects.

McCall signed a waiver of rights, and in his statement to Conway said that he and his young friend, fourteen-year-old David Orton, pulled under the bridge at 2:00 o'clock to "head to the top and watch for the train" that he "thought was heading their way." He stated that David, against his protests, took the paint can and began spraying it on the side of the train car that was already parked there. He further stated that he "walked off" because he "didn't approve and waited for him." He said that David then put the paint back in the car and they went on up to watch for the train. He said that it soon became apparent that the anticipated train was not coming after all, so about the time they got back to the car, Officer Weaver pulled up.

Young Orton refused to give a statement, so Weaver transported the two subjects to the Sherriff's Office in Manchester for warrants. Eighteen-year-old McCall was released on a $500.00 appearance bond, and Orton was handed over to his parents after the Juvenile Petition was served.

Would this latest arrest take care off our graffiti problem? The answer was "No."

Chapter Twenty-seven

Fortunately for us, the use of wires on Donnie Northcutt was never needed. We didn't have to wait much longer to uncover the real story.

It was in the wee morning hours of the next Thursday, April 3rd, when the genuine break came in the mysterious case of M.K. By now even the First Methodist Church and the Tennessee Tanning properties had been hit.

At least the public had paid attention to our ardent cries for help. A Vandalism call came in regarding a building on West Lincoln Street. The culprit had been caught in the act by the property owner! Officer Mike Blackburn was quickly on the scene and observed the suspect fleeing across the street as he was arriving. Dashing from his cruiser, Blackburn was able to overtake the suspect and apprehend him within minutes in the Kawasaki parking lot.

The suspect jerked his head and grunted. Blackburn removed a backpack from him and took out the contents—several telltale cans of spray paint.

"You're under arrest for Vandalism, and Resisting Arrest. Anything you say can and will be used against you in a court of law..."

The young suspect glared into the officer's eyes and grinned.

"You are entitled to a lawyer; if you can't afford a lawyer one will be appointed for you by the court."

Blackburn shoved the suspect into his cruiser and went to speak with the property owner.

"I need your name, please, so we can nail this guy. And a little information about what happened this morning."

"Sure. Herb Massey. I live right there in that house. I spotted this idiot out there painting those letters on my fence. I bet this is the guy you've been after!"

"Just what happened then? Did you have any conversation with this man?"

"Definitely! I got a call on my cell phone from my alarm company that a motion detector sensor had gone off on the rear lot of my property. I quietly went back and heard the hissing of a spray paint can, and could see a faint outline of that guy out there. I shouted at him to stop and I saw him running towards the rear of the property. I chased him as far as I could. At that point I called 911. After that he ran through a gate and said, 'do you see this?' With my flashlight I could see that he was coming at me with an open bladed knife. I picked up a rock and threw it at him. I think I hit him in the stomach; anyway, that's when he made a dash for it. He was running toward the pawn shop holding a big bag."

"Thanks for letting me know. I'm going to need you to come by the station and give me a statement, then testify at this guy's trial. "

"No problem. I want to keep this jerk off the street."

The suspect, 22-year-old Jared C. Newport, was now in for a new charge — Aggravated Assault.

Newport was transported to headquarters, IDed, fingerprinted, mug shot, and placed in the bull pen.

Massey came by and submitted a complete handwritten tableau on the incident.

Newport was a native of Tullahoma who had lived in St. Augustine, Florida for four years as a teen. According to Newport, he was planning on moving to Pennsylvania soon. He wrote out a statement denying any involvement in the Vandalism incidents, and telling us that he had only taken pictures of it.

Then my man arrived, loaded for bear.

"I'm Investigator Jason Kennedy. I've been assigned to your case."

Newport ducked his head.

"Okay, Newport. The more you cooperate, the easier it's gonna be on you," Kennedy said gruffly. "We know you're the one who's been causing havoc all over town for the past five months."

Newport lifted his head and let out a long sigh.

"How about it, Jared? We've put a lot of man hours and money into this case, including surveillance cameras. There's a lot of damage to property out there. If you don't cooperate I'm gonna throw the book at you. We've got an eye witness, you know."

"Alright." Newport's voice trailed downward, "I'm the one who's been doin' the M.K. graffiti."

Jared Newport then signed a full confession on the M.K. Vandalism cases, excluding other graffiti and those committed by Donnie Northcutt, along with an apology to the city and stating his willingness to help repair the damage 'in any way possible.'

Chapter Twenty-eight

This was by no means our first rash of Vandalism in Tullahoma, just the most concentrated and baffling. In 2006 alone we had had over 300 individual cases, with property damage to locals set at over $152,000.00. 2007 saw over 200 incidents with around $100,000.00 in damage, the first M.K. graffiti incident being among the last that year. But during this harrowing series of Vandalisms I learned a lot about dealing with this common problem for cities across America and around the globe in our crime-ravaged world.

Jared Newport was released under a $10,000 bond and ordered to appear in General Sessions Court on Thursday, April 24th at 9:00 A.M. Other charges remained pending.

His final trial date was November 29th, 2008, and he received a sentence of eleven months and twenty-nine days, which was suspended due to time served. His requirements of probation included restitution of cleaning up all of the graffiti which had not already been eradicated by the City of Tullahoma.

He still had plenty of work which undoubtedly gave him time to contemplate the seriousness of his crime and the money which he had cost the city.

Other charges against him—another count of unrelated Vandalism, Resisting Arrest, and Possession of a Firearm—were all dismissed pending satisfactory completion of the terms of his probation.

But there are Jared Newports in every city in America, and likely around the world, who are not sorry for their crimes until they are caught—like the two Worth Sporting Goods employees that we had apprehended who had been stealing bats, gloves and bags.

When we found their stash, shipping manager Dale Phillips needed a van to reclaim the enormous amount of merchandise that had been taken.

As in most cases, the perpetrators had been young adults. There were 29 high-tech softball bats recovered which retailed at about $200 each, plus the gloves and bags. The bats were being sold for $100 each in Shelbyville, Franklin County, and Kentucky. We had no idea how much merchandise had gone to Kentucky which could not be traced once it was out of state, and never recovered.

I had apprehended one of the suspects while he was escaping with some bats. The man's Volvo was impounded in which several bats were found. But the lion's share of the stash was discovered at his house. The auto of the other suspect, a late-model Ford was also impounded. And, oh yes, the men were found guilty and sentenced. But did they really regret their crimes, or simply the fact that they were caught?

Chapter Twenty-nine

Immediately following the trial of Jared Newport, our year-long study of a local drug cartel paid off. Together with the F.B.I., our department began our roundup of suspects.

The first phase of the investigation had begun in November of 2007, and had been labeled, "Operation Lockdown." I had put Sergeant Jason Ferrell and Investigator Dale Stone, two of my top men, in charge, and working with F.B.I. Special Agent Richard Poff. The aim: shut down the crack cocaine distribution in Tullahoma. They had discovered that there were eight key players in this vicious game.

Then in early December, 2008, arrests were carried out by strategic officers on our force and indictments were handed down by the Grand Jury against the five men and three women, aged between 24 and 53; the majority being in their mid-thirties. After their indictments, the eight were transported to Franklin County Jail (because it is certified to house federal prisoners) where they were held overnight before being transferred to Federal Court in Chattanooga and turned over to U.S. Marshalls.

Reflections of an Investigator

Along with the arrests, all eight of their vehicles and a Tullahoma residence being used as a 'crack house' were seized, as well as a stash of drugs and cash which had been taken in from the sales of the illegal coke operation.

Charges against those arrested ranged from possession of a controlled substance with intent to resell, to maintaining a crack house for the purpose of distributing crack cocaine and conspiracy to distribute crack cocaine.

As usual, I want to say that our officers and investigators did a marvelous job.

The feds did not let them get away with this, and I was proud that our department had been a major part of this important operation. But the problems with drugs, like death and taxes, continue to haunt Tullahoma and every city and county in the nation.

Chapter Thirty

Once again, Christmas came and went. My time with the family is so important to me. I treasure every minute with my beautiful wife, Linda, and my three lovely daughters. Leah and Yolanda are fairly close, but I don't get to see my oldest daughter, Shannon, as often as I would like due to the drive to Toledo being so long. I especially enjoyed getting to see her and her family, that year, though.

That January, 2009, a fifty-year-old Murfreesboro man was fatally shot by Coffee County deputies in a chase on I-24 near Manchester, after the suspect had pointed a nine millimeter pistol at them.

The county dispatcher had received a 911 call at 6:30 that morning from a woman who said that her ex-husband was following her vehicle on the interstate, and was "possibly armed." When the deputies and the Manchester Police had arrived on the scene, the woman had flashed her lights and her ex-husband had slowed his pickup truck. Police had gone ahead and placed spikes in his path, but the man had swerved and avoided hitting them.

After the suspect missed the third strip, and went into the medium, a Manchester officer fired a shot, hitting his left rear tire. From the report, the suspect then pulled to the shoulder of the interstate, exited the truck, and aimed a pistol at the deputies. He was struck by one bullet and pronounced dead at the scene.

In the meantime, less than a month after the cocaine arrests, Investigators Jason Ferrell, Ty Brazier, Jason Kennedy, Dale Stone, Harry Conway and I, along with Officers Robert Burns and George Marsh and School Resource Officer Joe Brown were busy with K-9 teams from several police agencies at the Tullahoma High School on a call informing us that illegal drugs were present. The dogs alerted on eight lockers, but those proved to contain no drugs, though there were indications that clothing in them had been in contact with illegal narcotics.

But we hit the jackpot in the parking lot. A total of 19 vehicles were alerted by the dogs, and we turned up one car containing alcohol, pot, and a great deal of drug paraphernalia. Another had a small amount of marijuana and some additional alcohol inside. As a result of the searches, five teens were charged; three as adults and two as juveniles.

But not all that happened in early 2009 was negative. That spring I was to make a new friend that would change my life.

Chapter Thirty-one

In April of 2009, I was attending a Scottish event in Murfreesboro—a Tartan Day celebration—with the Highland Rim Scottish Society. There, as I was walking about, checking out the tents, I found the Clan Sinclair tent and noticed that the gentleman manning it had some books displayed. I picked one up and flipped through it.

"Did you write this?" I asked, a wrinkle forming on my brow.

"Yes. I wrote all of these," came his reply. "I'm Stan St. Clair, Tennessee Commissioner for our clan," he continued, extending his hand.

"Ron Cunningham," I said, reaching for the shake. "I'm with the Scottish Society. We're right over there." I made a gesture toward our tent. "I think I'm going to take this one; it looks interesting. How much is it?"

He told me and I paid him.

"I've got a story that needs to be told," I said. "I've been waiting thirty years to get the right person to write it."

"Thirty years?" His tone was understandably filled with wonder.

Reflections of an Investigator

"Yes. I was the Sheriff of Moore County in the late '70s and early '80s, and there was a contract out on my life. They did a sting with the F.B.I., the T.B.I. and the A.T.F. and caught the conspirators."

"Wow! Why hasn't someone written this before?" Stan asked.

"I guess it just wasn't the right time," I said. "Some people asked for the book and movie rights when it happened, but they just wanted it for themselves."

"That's not right! I'd like to talk to you about it some time," he said.

"Sure, here's my card. I'm Captain of Investigations with the Tullahoma Police Department now."

Stan took my card, and I went back to my tent. A few days later he called me and wanted to get together. The rest is history. My friendship with Stan is now resulting in this book, the third and final volume in our 'true crime' series.

We would meet, first at his home, then at my office to go to lunch, or at my home to put together the material for *Conspiracy in the Town that Time Forgot*. We have spent many good times together that year, and in the years since, it has been time that I will never forget.

Stan and me at a book signing at Manchester Library, one of a great many signings that we have done.

Chapter Thirty-two

It was July of 2009 before Jeffrey Randall went to trial. The charge was Solicitation of Aggravated Statutory Rape, and Judge Vanessa Jackson was presiding

The morning was wearing on. The trial had started early, the case had been presented, material witnesses had been testifying; now the last non-officer had just been excused. The court asked for the next witness, which would be the final one. The prosecuting attorney called Harry Conway, and he was sworn in. The court reporter glared expressionless at his fingers as they fairly sang on the keys.

"Before we start," the Assistant D.A., Jason Ponder, frowned and stepped closer, "I noticed you took a notebook up there. You know you can't read from that, so don't try to read from your notebook."

"Yes, sir." Conway was trying not to meet the attorney's demanding gaze.

"Excuse me. Please state your name."

"My name is Harry Lee Conway, Jr."

"You are employed with the Tullahoma Police Department?"

"Yes, sir."

"What is your position there?"

"My title is Community Service Investigator. It's kind of a double role."

"You investigate child abuse cases?"

"Yes, sir. On the community services aspect, I actually go into schools, into the community, and do public presentations and that type of thing for the Police Department. For the investigations side, I handle child abuse, child neglect, sex abuse. I'm over the Sex Offender Registry, and I also handle the adult protective services with the Department of Human Services, same respect as with children."

"You were called out to investigate this case, right?" The attorney placed his hand on the railing and leaned in toward Conway.

"Yes, sir."

"Can you tell us about your initial call?"

Conway calmly related his experience being given the call by his sergeant/supervisor, Jason Ferrell, and being asked to go to D.W. Wilson Center to investigate.

"Okay. Did you do that?"

"Yes, sir."

"D.W. Wilson, that recreation center, that is located where?"

"It's on Collins, North Collins Street in Tullahoma. It is in Coffee County, just south of Wilson Avenue and east of Cedar Lane."

"All right. When you arrived at the center, who was there?"

"When I arrived, I entered through the main doors and went into the office areas, which are, as you are looking at the building at that time, the right portion of the building. I entered the office area and spoke to Joe Brown, Mr. Glick. J. P Kraft was there, and Zack Pane and Jeb Brand were there.

Okay. Did you have an opportunity to speak to all of them?"

"Yes, sir."

"All right. Without getting into all the details all over again—the jury has heard these multiple times—was it reported to you what has been reported in court today?"

"Yes, sir."

"What were the first steps, or what were *your* first steps in your investigation process?"

"The first phase of it, I was introduced to what had occurred, and then once I had found this out, I asked some questions of the two boys. I was getting statements from them, and spoke to Tara Pane and..."

"Statements... I'm sorry to interrupt," Ponder interjected, "but the statements you mentioned, are those the written statements the boys made out?"

"Yes, sir."

"They have been submitted into evidence?"

"Yes, sir."

"Okay, go ahead."

"Once I got the written statements from the two boys, Jeb and Zack Pane—Jeb Brand—this was after I asked them what had happened, I spoke to Al Brand and Tara Pane and kind of inquired about their background—had they had any problems from the teenagers, that type of thing, their academics, and I was asserting—trying to ascertain if their credibility would be..."

"Objection, Your Honor," Perry Craft, the defense attorney spoke up.

"You want to rephrase or...?" Judge Jackson asked with a bit of apprehension in her distinctive voice.

"He just said he was trying to make a determination as to their credibility from his prospective. I don't think that..." Ponder stated in a matter-of-fact tone.

"What is your objection, Mr. Craft?" the judge came back.

"I think he is trying to bolster their credibility, and it hasn't...I haven't attacked it, and he is doing it through hearsay, Your Honor, not what he has talked to people about. That is just not proper."

"I didn't hear any hearsay statements," the judge asserted.

"No." Ponder said, a smug simper forming on his face.

"I will allow it."

"Okay," Ponder continued, "you got, suffice it to say, you got some background information; right?"

"Yes, sir." Conway was finally allowed to regain the conversation.

"What did you do next?"

"Once I got the statements and spoke to their parents, I spoke to Mr. Glick and Mr. Kraft, and we were—at that time, they had already reviewed some of the video and knocked some of the names off of the roster from the contractors, so they kind of narrowed the names down, and there were several names we were looking at and I was focused in on, and I received the video...."

The discourse went on and it seemed to Conway that no one was even hearing him. Then he saw that the jurors were once again tuned in as he said, "...and he actually focused in on the areas on the video where I could observe any activity between Mr. Randall and the two boys...I had a pretty good look at Mr. Randall via the video footage....I attempted to identify Randall. We looked up the roster and it said, "Wayne Randall." As an investigator I have access to the State of Tennessee's driver's license data base system, so what I did, I pulled up all of the Wayne Randalls statewide, and what I had determined was there were hardly any of those names, and the photos didn't match—the driver's license photos didn't match the surveillance video, so what I had assumed was Wayne was a middle name, so I pulled up, and we narrowed it finally down to two or three Jeffrey Wayne Randalls in Tennessee."

"Suffice it to say," Ponder said, "you eventually identified the individual that came in contact with Zack Pane on that video, is that right?"

"Yes, sir. I used the video, the driver's license, and the signature on the roster and the license, and we narrowed it down that way."

The questioning continued concerning the video, with Conway showing superb confidence.

Finally, Ponder looked Conway deep in his eyes. "From your review of the video, do we have today, and have we introduced into evidence, all the video pertains to this defendant coming into contact with and being around the two boys that day?"

"Yes, sir."

After specifically identifying the time frame as being that of the alleged sexual insinuation, Conway was questioned about his talk with the boys' parents.

"What did you do next?"

"At that point I made a determination of an arrest warrant, but prior to that, I did make contact with Mr. Randall at his employment...and spoke to him on the phone, and did verify the information on his driver's license with what I had. Everything matched, and then I went and got the arrest warrant and myself and Jason Kennedy, an investigator with the Tullahoma Police Department, actually drove down to his residence to pick up Mr. Randall on the warrant.

"Did you tell Mr. Randall on the phone that you were coming to arrest him?"

"No, sir."

"How much time passed between the time you talked to him on the phone and the time you went?"

"I spoke to Mr. Randall on the phone between 3:00 and 4:00 and Jason Kennedy and I left about 5:00. We coordinated with the Lawrence County Sheriff's Department to meet us at the address, and it was about between 7:30 and 8:00 when we actually got there."

"What did you do when you got to his residence?"

"When we arrived we attempted to make contact with Mr. Randall. We did make contact with his wife at that time. She was alone at the residence. She advised us that Mr. Randall and his two children were at a church function, and we waited. During that time period, I had an occasion to talk with Mrs. Randall to go over the reasons why we were there.

"What did you tell her?"

"I explained to Mrs…"

"Objection, Your Honor!" Craft snapped. "It is an out-of-court statement."

"Relevance, General Ponder?" the judge's eyes widened.

"We are going to, if we may approach?"

"Ladies and gentlemen, if you will excuse us for a few minutes."

The jury exited the courtroom. Slight mumbles arose from the audience.

Chapter Thirty-three

I was glad I had other things to do while Harry Conway was at the Randall trial, but I would soon be briefed about the proceedings.

There were always new challenges. One thing that was peaking about then was final proofs and editing of *Conspiracy in the Town That Time Forgot*. So many people were supporting this effort: all of my family who wanted the story to be told and a myriad of my friends in law enforcement and the legal professions. Assistant D.A., Emily Roberts, was extremely helpful in the final process, for which I want to thank her again at this time.

But the trial went on. Assistant District Attorney General Jason M. Ponder was determined that he was going to get the whole story out in the open and keep Wayne Randall from attempting to prey on young boys.

After the jury had left the court room, Judge Jackson asked the lawyers to be seated.

"First, if you will explain the relevance, and then we will get his objection," she said to Ponder in a firm tone.

"Your Honor, the relevance is her reaction when she is advised of the nature of this crime that is being alleged."

"How is that relevant?"

"How is her reaction relevant?"

"Yes."

"Perhaps it is not. I thought the objection was hearsay,"

The judge frowned. "I said before we got to that, 'Relevance.' Tell me how it is relevant."

"Well, Your Honor, the defendant had been advised that the police were coming."

"Okay."

"The defendant was not at home."

"I thought he said he didn't advise him that he was going to be arrested."

"Not that he was going to be arrested, but that the police—I didn't really go into that as to how much…"

"I didn't hear him say the police were coming," the judge cut him off.

Ponder was quick to respond. "Mr. Randall was aware that the police had called him."

"Okay." The judge nodded.

"Roughly two hours before the police arrived at his home. It certainly can be inferred that he told his wife something or that something had gone on there. I don't know." Ponder was shaking his head slowly. "Certainly we can skip past this if you feel uncomfortable, Your Honor, but I can give you the evidence and let you make the determination based on the answers if you like. We have no jury here."

"Yes, that would probably be the best thing to do."

With the jury still absent, Ponder continued with his questions to Harry Conway, and began by returning to his discussion with Mrs. Randall while waiting on her husband to return. He had explained to her the charges against her husband and the fact that they were there to arrest him.

"She asked me a question, 'Was it a boy or a girl?' I kind of paused for a second. I was like — I was thinking through my mind, 'Why was she asking this question?'

"He had then informed her that he was not at liberty to relate the age or the sex of the juvenile, only the fact that the victim was a juvenile.

"Then I kind of saw a puzzled look—she had an expression. I don't know if she was angry or what the expression was, but I asked her, I said, 'Have you ever noticed or observed any kind of unusual activity with Mr. Randall over the years?' She kind of ignored my question. We spoke of something else, then I asked the question once more, and her response was, 'I just don't want to talk about it.'"

"This is why I asked the jury to go out. I knew this was where we were headed. Now we are getting dangerously close to prior acts, are we not?"

After a bit more discourse, Ponder said, "What I found particularly odd...first off, her reaction was not one of shock, and that she only had one question, 'Was it a boy or a girl?' That is specifically what I feel is relevant."

The investigation had turned up a twenty-year old conviction against the suspect, and it was not admissible—the judge questioned Ponder's intent in his line of questioning Conway.

Then Craft spoke up.

"Your Honor, here is what we are trying to do here. First of all, his own testimony was he didn't say he was coming to arrest him."

"Okay."

Craft continued, "As a matter of fact, the..."

"Hang on just a second!" the judge said, cutting him short.

"I apologize, Your Honor." *Can she read my mind?*

"Go ahead. The door will close, it is going slow, but it will close."

"And she is not the defendant," Craft injected.

"Okay," the judge nodded.

"All right," Craft continued, "so what we are trying to do is get what other people said, dah, dah, dah. The question is, what did Randall do? What didn't he do? And if we bring in some extraneous kinds of things, we are bringing prejudicial comments that all of a sudden start inviting and opening the door for further speculation. Let's try Randall on what happened on November 21st -- what he said — what he did, not what other people did or didn't do. The court was right."

"Are you arguing that what was said in the home was hearsay?" The judge's look was stern.

"I'm sorry, Your Honor, I didn't say it is hearsay..."

"No, you didn't. I'm just asking."

"I'm arguing both relevance and hearsay, Your Honor,"

"All right. Reaction of bystanders at an arrest, General Ponder, tell me again why you think it is relevant."

"Your Honor, this is the defendant's wife. There is no one more, I suppose, privy to his nature. This falls under what I kind of think of as tacit admission when someone is faced with an allegation, and their reaction is not one that is, I suppose, what society would think is normal. It has seen under the law oftentimes as tacit admission. No statement need be made..."

"Now we are talking about not the defendant. We're talking about his wife."

"That's true," Ponder admitted.

"Okay, I don't think the spousal doctrine goes that far. If spouses can do tacit admissions on their spouses, we are in trouble."

More tense conversation followed; then the judge reiterated her position.

"We are getting dangerously close to prior bad acts. I'm going to say this one more time. Her knowledge of what he has done in the past, is that not bad prior acts?"

Reflections of an Investigator

"I think specific prior bad acts under the rule cannot be admitted. I am not asking to do that. I realize there are some other implications that come out of this testimony. Otherwise, I wouldn't offer it, but I do not believe this rises to the level of using prior bad acts to impeach character or prove anything. This is just her reaction to an allegation made against this man that she has been married to for years."

"Well," the judge rubbed her chin and sighed, "I don't mean to pick a fight with you, but you are double arguing. You are arguing that you are not offering it for something, and then you told me why you are arguing it."

"I offer everything for something," Ponder said frankly. "The hearsay rule doesn't apply because a question by its nature is not hearsay. Now under the relevancy, obviously, I'm offering it for something. I realize it is not, quote 'a tacit admission,' precisely but it is akin to that. I can call her to the stand to explain it, but I think it infers some knowledge on her part that she did not offer. She is not entitled to Miranda. She can't claim the right to remain silent. I think if we didn't have this twenty-year-old conviction we wouldn't be having this discussion. This is not our attempt to back door this in."

"I understand," the judge sighed as if a weight had been lifted.

"That is not what this is about — this is her reaction to a statement that was made to her and how odd that reaction was, given the light of the surrounding circumstances."

"I'm going to allow it up to the point where she asks if it was a boy or a girl; but no other conversation after that where you were asking about 'what you have seen in the past.' Mr. Craft," The judge turned and addressed the defense attorney, "I will give you a chance to rebut. I think that it is obviously bad prior acts."

"Yes, Your Honor," Ponder said in a low tone.

Chapter Thirty-four

Before the jury was called back, Craft began a hypothetical cross-examination, feeling the judge's temperature regarding an admissible line of questioning; citing restrictions under sections 403, 404, and 609, to make certain that he would not be the cause of a similar halting of the trial. Once the ground rules were squarely in place, Judge Jackson called a five-minute break to make a phone call, and then the jury was allowed to return to the courtroom.

"Be seated, go ahead, General," Judge Jackson said, as if there had been no interruption.

"Thank you, Your Honor," Ponder said, turning to Conway.

"You went to the defendant's home in Lawrence County. He was not home, correct?"

"Yes, sir."

However, his wife was home?"

"Yes, sir."

"And you had a conversation with her in the beginning?"

"Yes, sir."

"She inquired as to what the nature of your visit was, is that right?"

"Yes, sir."

"You gave her some detail. What did you say?"

"I told Mrs. Randall that we were there to arrest her husband for Solicitation to Commit Aggravated Statutory Rape. Mrs. Randall wanted to inquire as far as to the exact details. I told her that I could not explain everything to her. I kind of gave her the highlights, and then at one point, Mrs. Randall asked me a question—'Was it a girl or a boy?'"

"Objection, Your Honor!" Craft said, popping to his feet.

"Yes, sir?" the judge said, a tad of irritation in her voice.

"Your Honor, may I approach the bench?"

"My Craft," the judge said firmly, "we have already talked about this. I said I would allow *this*, okay?"

Craft lowered his head. "Okay."

"This is what I'm going to allow."

Craft nodded briskly and mutely returned to his seat.

Ponder's face muscles loosened and an aura of satisfaction replaced the grimace that had pervaded his features for the past few intense moments. Though he couldn't go further, he had gotten a valuable point over to the jury.

"Officer Conway, did you wait for the defendant to come home?"

"Yes, sir."

"By the way, you didn't give her any more detail, did you?"

Craft's instincts peaked. "Objection, Your Honor!"

Ponder grinned inside. "Well, never mind. That's fine. That's not really that big a deal."

The judge remained mute.

Ponder continued. "You waited for the defendant to come home?"

"Yes, sir."

"How long did you have to wait?"

"Mrs. Randall advised us that they were at a church function, and it shouldn't be much longer, so the two deputies—well, Mrs. Randall advised us that it probably would be better if our presence wasn't known, so we placed the two Lawrence

County deputies in an adjacent driveway to watch for Mr. Randall to arrive, while Mr. Kennedy and myself moved our car—or he moved his car—to a location behind the house. We waited, I want to say, roughly twenty minutes, and all three arrived; and at that point, when Mr. Randall exited his vehicle—I think he was in a pickup truck—once he exited the vehicle, I advised him that he was under arrest, and for what reason."

"What did you do next?"

"Placed handcuffs on Mr. Randall, and at that point, Mrs. Randall advised the two children—it might have been just prior to that, but just about that time—to enter the house and not come out. We spoke to Mr. Randall outside and placed him in the back seat of Mr. Kennedy's patrol vehicle— unmarked investigators vehicle—advised Mr. Randall of his Miranda warning—or his Miranda rights and then allowed Mrs. Randall and Mr. Randall to speak very briefly, and then we left.

"Did you have at some point a conversation with the defendant about what happened?"

"Yes, sir. Once we were inside the vehicle and I was sitting in the back seat with Mr. Randall, while Mr. Kennedy was driving the vehicle, we were en route back to Tullahoma. I spoke to Mr. Randall about the reason for his arrest in a detailed nature.

But just prior to that, he asked me, 'What is this about? The photographs? The pictures?' And not too long after that is when I advised him, 'No, it was in reference to solicitation of a minor to commit aggravated rape. He denied it, and his conversation while traveling was that he never spoke to anybody that was under the age of 18, not directly in that format. He said he didn't speak to any of the kids up there who were playing. Intermittently he would jump in and talk about the weather or talk about law enforcement working different shifts and things like that. But he denied any kind of contact or anything associated with the allegation.

"Was he pretty conversational with you?" Ponder asked.

"Yes, sir."

"Now at some point a written statement was given, is that right?"

"Yes, sir. I advised Mr. Randall, or asked him, actually, if he would submit a written statement regarding what he had told me in the presence of Mr. Kennedy in the vehicle. Once we got back to the Tullahoma Police Department, we went into my office, and I allowed Mr. Randall to sit down and write out the statement of what he had explained to us in the vehicle while traveling.

"Your Honor," Ponder turned to Judge Jackson, "may I approach?"

"Yes, sir."

"Can you identify this document, please?" Ponder said, handing it to Officer Conway.

"That is a photocopy of the statement Mr. Randall made to me on that evening at the Police Department in my office."

"Okay. On the back of that is the Miranda form?"

"Yes, sir."

"Did he execute that form?"

"He did," Conway said with a nod, "yes, sir."

"In front of you?"

"Yes, sir."

"Back on the side containing his statement, were those his words or your words."

"Those were his words. He actually—I wrote out the actual beginning of the statement, talking about the name, sex, race, etc. Then there is an actual block within the statement—I allowed Mr. Randall to write it himself. Once he completed the statement in written format, I asked him questions, and I wrote the questions and his answers out below his statement within the same block."

"Let me ask you something. At this point, when you were asking those questions and recording his answers, had you informed him that there was a video at this point?"

"At this point, no."

"Read us the first question that you asked him, the specific question."

"Yes, sir."

"Your Honor," Craft spoke up, "I'm going to object. I think it speaks for itself. He is highlighting one point of the document."

"I'm going to submit the entire document, Your Honor," Ponder stated.

"Well then," Mr. Craft is right," the judge said, clearing her throat. "The document speaks for itself. You may ask him what question he asked, and if he doesn't remember, he can look at the document to refresh his recollection, but to have him read the document, I believe, is not the correct way to do it."

"You are correct, Your Honor. At this time I would ask that this be moved into evidence as the next State's exhibit."

"So admitted."

The document was marked and entered into evidence as Exhibit 10. Ponder verified that the document was complete, and that it contained the defendant's statement. Then he continued to ask about specific portions before passing it to the jury, asking if it had been completed before Randall had been told of the video. An affirmative answer was given.

Ponder again asked Conway to read aloud from the document, which was disallowed by the Court, and the document was passed to the jury. The judge only stated that the rules must be followed.

One of the specific questions, Conway stated, was whether or not Randall had come in contact with anyone under the age of 18 at the center. The explanations continued. The jury shifted, and some were looking at their watches. They had already heard these questions.

Finally, Ponder looked squarely into Conway's eyes. "Did you then tell him he was on video?"

"Yes, sir, and how I did it was, I showed Mr. Randall the actual arrest warrant, and in the warrant the affiant, which would have been myself, explained the reason I requested the warrant, and within the narrative, it explains that his activities were observed on—well, they were on videotape. When Mr. Randall read that in the arrest warrant, he became very—well pretty irate at that time and said, 'Videotape? What videotape?' At that point, he just quit talking. He wouldn't respond to any of my questions."

Ponder nodded and smiled at Craft. "All right. Thank you, your witness."

Chapter Thirty-five

Craft ambled slowly to the front of the courtroom.

"I believe you indicated that when you first saw Mr. Randall was that night after he got back from church with his kids, is that right?"

"He arrived home by himself, but his children were in another vehicle, and they arrived, I think, just prior to his arrival, but it was almost simultaneous, I believe."

"Did you see him get out of his pickup truck?"

"I'm fairly certain it was his work vehicle, yes, sir."

"Did it have Claxton Construction on the work vehicle?"

"It had some kind of writing. I honestly didn't pay attention to what it said."

"Did you see the telephone number on the back of it?"

"I don't recall."

"You don't recall that? Do you recall if he had on a shirt that night?" Snickers arose through the courtroom, and the judge banged her gavel. "Did he have on a shirt?" Craft repeated.

"Mr. Randall was still wearing the attire that was visible on the surveillance video."

"Did it have the Claxton Construction logo on it, do you *recall* that?"

"It had some kind of logo on it, but I wasn't paying attention to that part."

"You were with him for *how long* that night?"

"From around 8:00 to somewhere around 11:00 that evening."

"That's about three hours or more?"

"Roughly, yes, sir."

"All right, now the truck, when you first saw him, was a Chevy Truck, wasn't it?"

"I can't recall. I remember it being a light colored vehicle or pickup truck. I want to say either white or cream color; I'm not for sure."

"Do you think it might have been brown, or do you recall?"

"It could have been brown," Conway twisted his mouth, "it was dark that night, yes, sir."

"You believe it was a company truck, don't you?"

"I believe it was his work vehicle. I believe he made that statement or something to that effect."

More trivial conversation about the arrest, the vehicle and the trip to and from Randall's home seemed to drag needlessly through the afternoon. A juror was nodding, apparently wondering when this trivial pursuit would end. *Where were the objections now?*

Chapter Thirty-six

The dozing juror lifted his head and tossed back his graying black hair. He gazed at his watch rubbing the sleep from his eyes.

The pre-bid sign-in sheet at the D.W. Wilson Center on which Randall's name had been scrawled that fateful day was being discussed. Craft petitioned the court for a copy, which was already in evidence. The request easily was granted.

"For the purpose of the record, may I state, I believe everybody is through looking at that statement. Is that not the case?" Judge Jackson frowned.

The juror who dosed noticed that the others were shaking their heads in the negative.

The judge allowed Ponder to read it aloud, but refused to permit it to enter the jury room.

Craft asked to approach the bench.

"Would you look at page 2 of exhibit Number 1, line 3, please? There is a name, would you read that name?"

"The name on the line is Randall."

The signature matched that on Randall's driver's license. The next line showed the name of Randall's company, which the judge was also asked to read. The phone number was also present. The judge reluctantly agreed to have it passed to the jury. *Why was the defense attorney doing this?*

But there was a method to his 'madness.' The amount of money to be spent on the project, it turned out, was around $2,000,000. Nothing to be sneezed at. Would a contractor, or even a subcontractor, risk it all on such a matter? Conway was not a contractor. His knowledge of this field was minimal, right? Craft continued his powerful drilling of the officer, questioning his handling of the arrest.

Finally Judge Jackson brought the line of questioning to a halt and demanded that Craft move on.

Craft then concentrated on the cameras, their angles and their ability to scan the entire gym, bringing out another exhibit—a drawing of the interior of the gym at the Wilson Center, proving his point.

Questioning led back to the arrest. Then full-circle to the Center and the video. He also mentioned 'facts' of which Conway could not have been aware, and asked questions to which he could only reply, "I don't recall." His tactics were continuously demanding. Craft left no stone unturned as he waded through his cross-examination—even those which had seemed to gather moss along the way.

The day dragged painfully on. A nervous female juror wondered if she could hold out till a break to use the rest room. Other exhibits were brought out, including, Exhibit 4A, one of two burned DVDs which were a copy of portions of the surveillance video. Craft asked to view part of the video in court.

"Ladies and gentlemen, you can take about a ten minute break," Judge Jackson said. The jury filed out.

Ah, relief!

Chapter Thirty-seven

The judge questioned the attorneys as to their course of further action, whether the sign-in document and video would be admissible to the jury, and 'hoops to jump through,' including Ponder's possible re-direct of Conway.

Craft asked permission for Randall to have a short break, which the court allowed.

Court rules were discussed and interest questioned. The judge finally agreed to allow the video.

After the jury was brought back in, the screen was positioned to allow both Conway and the jurors to have adequate view.

"Now this is a depiction of the gym that you saw that day?" Craft asked, nodding toward the witness.

"Yes, sir."

"I want you to look at this area right here in the paint. Do you see that?"

"The darker area?"

"Would you agree that is the foul line?"

Reflections of an Investigator

"I'm not familiar with basketball, I'm sorry."

"Do you see this area that is whitish here?"

"There is a lighter area that is within the darker area, yes, sir."

"The paint had faded, is that your understanding, or do you know?"

"I don't know, no sir."

"All right. I will play the video in various segments."

Conway nodded.

"If you will watch the timer with me, I will stop it. Did you see how it skipped from 15:01 to 15:09?"

"Yes, sir."

"There it is at the 13. What happened between 15:13 and 15:49?"

"You have a skip of numbers on your time." Conway looked up with a slight smirk on his face.

"Do you think it was fast forwarded or do you think there is a skip there?"

"I was given to understand that their system updates itself. It doesn't continuously record. It's based on a sensory part of it that records only when it sees movement. That enables it to conserve space on the original recording."

Conway was trying to hold back making obvious his knowledge that he was not being outwitted.

"Do you see here near the back doors? Do you see that?"

"The double doors?"

"Yes, sir."

"Yes, sir."

One of the jurors let out a tiny chuckle, feeling like he was watching a scene from *Spies Like Us*.

"Does that appear to be two people there?"

"From where I'm sitting it looks like there is *some* individual."

"I want you to look from 10:50 to 10:56. I'm sorry, let me stop it. Let's do from 10:00 to 10:17. It goes immediately, doesn't it? It skips or fast forwards?"

"It skips numbers, yes, sir," Conway nodded his head in agreement.

"You see two people in the gym?"

"Yes, sir."

"There is motion going on there, isn't there?"

"There is."

"During that nine seconds, there is motion; is that right?"

"Are you talking about between the numbers?" Conway wrinkled his brow.

"Yes, sir, yes, sir. Is that the way it appears to you, or do you know?"

"From what I could tell on the video I could see the numbers jumping, and I see the motion..."

"...I'm sorry. I didn't mean to interrupt you."

"I'm sorry, I was just replying. I see activity on the cameras, and the numbers you're talking about jumping."

"Did you see this person all the way from here to there lickety-split because of the skip or fast forward?"

"Yes, sir."

Craft continued directing Conway to a specific location.

"What happened there?"

"Jump of numbers and activity."

"Can you tell if anyone is back here," Craft pointed, "at the door?"

"There was. Just ran south, I believe, the way the building sets."

"Then there was motion going on that the camera didn't pick up?"

"Between the numbers?"

"Yes, sir."

"It didn't show any activity. I just saw the motion where the individual ran."

"We started about 10:17:13. We ended up about 10:`19:14. Would you agree? I can replay if you like."

"10:17 to 19. I can agree with that."

A smug look rested on the attorney's face. "That's a minute and 42 seconds. Does that sound about right to you?"

Conway nodded. "Approximately, yes, sir."

Craft again questioned about the motion not displayed.

"It doesn't show any motion, but I couldn't see what was *not* there."

Craft asked for permission and ran the clip again, addressing the court. "You ought to see me with home videos, Judge. I'm not that good."

Then turning toward the jury, he continued, "Now you see, people?"

Conway was annoyed, but tried to remain cool. "From what I observed between 10:17 and 10:19, the difference is, you are seeing different images and different activities and different time periods. That's what I'm observing, the boys playing basketball."

A conversation followed about the identification of individuals on the video. Craft sited the time on the clock, asking the officer to note it.

"Can you tell me what happened in roughly those twenty seconds just by looking at the video?" Craft asked.

"By looking at the video," Conway repeated, "you asked me to look at the time…"

Again the segment was replayed.

"What happened?" Craft bellowed. "The fact is, it's kind of hard to tell what's going on in places on that video, isn't it?"

"It doesn't depict the difference in what happened in time—what happened in that time period. I can't see what it's not showing. It shows the differences between, say, 10:19:36; what that image is with that activity, and then if you backed it up to 10:19:16, wasn't it?"

Now the monkey was on the attorney's back.

"Yes."

"The activity of that time period doesn't show here. I can't comment on what is not showing."

What if I told you there was another skip between 10:19:43 and 10:20:05? Do you want to see that?"

"I understand this principle. As I said, it was explained to me at the center."

"Do you recall what I showed you at 10:21:56? Or was that too fast for you?"

"To what are you referring?"

"I'm sorry, I'll try again," the attorney said. "I'm going to 10:20:18."

"10:20."

"Or thereabouts, yes, sir."

Momentarily Craft spoke up again. "Did you see that skip?"

"Yes, sir."

"What happened during that minute and 18 seconds, with regard to motion?"

Conway rubbed his chin gently with his left hand. "I was concentrating on the time, not the activity."

"Are you saying that it's pretty hard to tell where the motion is going on?"

"I'm having a hard time doing both."

"Can you tell how many people are at that door?"

"Looks like one in front of the double doors."

Craft's hand cast a shadow over the screen as he motioned toward it. "Okay, do you know what this is right there?"

"What are you pointing to, a little black spot in the corner?"

"I'll be very precise. Can you see the bleachers along the wall?"

"Yes, sir."

"Do you see the little black line catty-cornered from where the camera is on the wall? Do you know what that is?"

"It should be another camera. Yes, there was one there, with protection over it, to guard it from basketballs. But that camera was inoperable."

"You think that is the camera?"

"Yes, sir," Conway confirmed, "from this angle it seems so."

"Who would know if the camera was operable?"

"I would presume the staff."

"The staff?"

"Yes, sir. Mr. Kraft or Mr. Moon — one of them advised me that camera was inoperable on that particular day."

"Would Mr. Kraft have better knowledge than you?"

"Of course."

"Let's go to the next one. 10:22:37 to 53. What happened there?"

"It looks like a skip in numbers again."

Reflections of an Investigator

"Did it look like there were people in the gym during the skip?"

"While I was watching the numbers, peripheral vision showed me, it looked like the two boys were playing basketball there, but it was different images."

"Let me ask you this, do you see this person in the far corner under the other camera?"

"I see a *shape* over there."

"Does it look like a person to you?"

"It *could be*, yes, sir."

"Do you think that what he is looking at is blueprints? You *do* know what blueprints are, right?"

Conway felt a bit insulted. "I *know* what blueprints are, yes, sir."

"Do those look like blueprints folded on the floor?"

"I can't tell what he is looking at, if it even is a he or a she. From where I'm sitting it isn't at all clear."

"Tell me how many males and how many females are in the video. Do you know that?"

"At what point, sir?"

"During the whole video, how many males and females?

"There were different people in the gym area. I don't recall exactly...I mean the majority were male, but I can't pick out specifically without reviewing the entire video.

"Were there females?"

"I think there were in the gym area."

"Were there any in the hallway, do you recall?" If you don't recall..."

"...At one point, there were one or two females. I think one was Alisha Snell from the City of Tullahoma. I remember seeing her at one point."

"Any others that you recall?"

"I believe there was one blonde."

"All right, sir, that's fair enough. Let's go to some other skips."

Perry Craft then turned Conway's attention to these. Conway conceded that they did exist. *What did this matter?*

Finally the judge spoke up. "How many more skips have you got?"

"Your Honor, I've got 71 of these," Craft said matter-of-factly.

A rumble arose in the courtroom and jurors sighed.

"I think this is getting a little ridiculous. He is not a technician, or an expert. We don't have to go through all of these. Just show him the document, if the State has no objection to that."

"Actually, Your Honor, I was about to...we would be happy to stipulate there are various skips," Ponder said with an air of relief.

"Thank you very much," the judge breathed softly. "If you will put that into evidence, I will appreciate it."

Chapter Thirty-eight

The document was placed into evidence marked Exhibit 12, the court accepted it as evidence, and the trial continued. Once again some jurors were looking at their wrists in hopes that lunch break was imminent.

The gaps were accepted by all as filming skips rather than omitted fast-forwards artificially made.

Then the actions of Randall were brought up by Craft.

"Did you see in that portion any waving by Mr. Randall?"

"No, sir."

"Did you see him beckon to anyone in the gym, some kind of signal to come over or anything like that?"

"No, sir."

"Did you see that anywhere in either of these two videos?"

"Anywhere?"

"In the videos."

"Of Mr. Randall?"

Reflections of an Investigator

"Yes, doing this," the attorney used his index finger to make a wiggling motion, "or using his arms to motion anyone to come to him?"

"At this particular angle, I did not see that, no, sir."

"Did you see it in any video you saw that day?"

"Not that I recall. The actual motioning, no, sir."

"May I switch out the disc, Your Honor?"

"Okay."

"Mr. Ponder is the technical person here. I have my children to do it. Do you mind, Your Honor?"

Exhibit 4A was removed from the player, and Number 4B inserted.

"Your Honor," Craft said wryly, "I told you 71 skips before, I believe there are actually 88. I just didn't have the second page with me. If the State wouldn't mind letting me put that in a second page to Exhibit 12."

"Stipulation to the skips...yes, sir."

After adding the page, Craft apologized and continued. "I am going over a few of these, Your Honor, but I will be very brief."

The judge conceded, but with an understanding that it was covered by the stipulation.

As the questioning of Harry Conway continued, the middle-aged drowsy juror nodded off again, his head bobbing. He would occasionally jerk and hear something else about the skips in the video, then a discussion about the restrooms in the center. Then he heard Conway agree to the skips and the court admit a document as Exhibit 13. A bit later he heard a discussion of a male with a hat and a white shirt facing the double doors in the gym, and Mr. Randall facing the camera in the hallway.

Other marked exhibits were brought out. *How much longer could this take?* Again the conversation centered around the video which had resumed.

Finally it came to the part when the subject and the victim met. The video was played and replayed. Zoomed and paused. Craft continued to drill the officer about positions and angles. No sound, of course, would leave a lot to the imagination. Timing of Randall's arrival and departure were discussed. Randall's statement was again brought up. *He had denied contact with the victim.* Then the arrest and Harry Conway's position on the way back to Tullahoma, next to Randall in the back seat, and the speed of the car, even to the clothing worn by the defendant. *What did that have to do with the price of eggs in China?* the juror wondered.

But Conway maintained his cool regardless of the nature of the questioning. The attorney was apparently attempting to show that this had been a long day, and insinuate that judgment could have been blurred. Good tactics, no doubt, on his part.

Then Conway was questioned about the length of his personal service and the number of cases he had handled—how many times he had testified in court. Had he been in front of the Grand Jury? Federal courts? The answers were all affirmative. There was an effort by the defense attorney again to bring into doubt the ability of the officer to recall particulars of a given case.

Still Conway was unwavering in his resolve and his demeanor.

Again, the juror nearly drifted off to sleep. But he had heard enough. Ample evidence had been presented. The rest would be brought out in the jury room anyway.

Conway was finished. Court was recessed for lunch.

After lunch the attorneys wrapped up their statements to the jury and they retired to deliberate.

After hours of deliberation, the haggard jury re-entered the courtroom.

"Have you reached a verdict?"

"We have, Your Honor." The chairman handed the slip to the bailiff who passed it to Judge Jackson.

"So say you all?"

"Yes, Your Honor."

"You may read the verdict."

Randall stood motionless as the reading proceeded.

"On the charge of Solicitation of Aggravated Statutory Rape, we find the defendant, guilty."

A tear ran down the cheek of Randall's wife.

Wayne Randall was subsequently sentenced 120 days and granted work release.

The case seemed significant because a number of laws were examined, and a verdict reached which seemed appropriate, though little time was served, the Sex Offense Register notifies the public on these offenders, and that can't be bad.

Chapter Thirty-nine

I was sitting home with my wife on the evening of September 23, 2010 watching The Mentalist on TV. It had come on at 9:00 P.M.

That day I had read the email from my good friend Joe Wells that I mentioned in Chapter One. My mind had been fleeting back over the past thirty-three years that I had spent in law enforcement and how much I could relate to that officer.

About half way through The Mentalist, My cell phone began ringing. I was tempted to just let my voice mail answer it and check it after the show had finished. But for some reason, I felt compelled to grab it and say 'hello.'

"Hey, Ron, it's Paul."

Chief of Police Blackwell calling me at home always got my attention.

"A 26-year-old Manchester woman and her two young kids have been murdered. The Sheriff called me and asked me to assist in locating a suspect. His name is Michael Pearlman..."

My eyelids went up. "That name sounds familiar..."

"It should; he's a 30-year-old army recruiter here in Tullahoma. The lady who was killed, Serena Hoffman, was his girlfriend. They found her body and those of her kids stuffed in plastic garbage bags in a closet in her home. They've been dead several days."

Cold chills ran over my spine like cascading water ripples. *How could anyone do something like this?* Yet such things happen a lot more often than we like to think about.

Before I could respond, he continued. "Notify all of your investigators."

"You got it. I'm on this!" I said.

I dressed in my call-out uniform, jumped in my Ford Expedition (which I had confiscated from a local drug dealer), switched on my blue lights and sped toward headquarters.

I called a couple of my investigators en route and told them to get hold of the others.

As I entered the Tullahoma city limits, my police radio was feeding me the latest on Pearlman. His motorcycle had been spotted in front of a room at Jameson Inn just down the street from the station.

By the time my men and I arrived at the scene, the motel was already surrounded by members of various law enforcement agencies, including the TBI.

I hastily donned my bullet-proof vest and darted upstairs where the Sheriff and his deputies were posted. Michael Pearlman had barricaded himself in his room.

"Sheriff," I said calmly, the logical approach would be for us to first shut off all the lights on and around the building."

The Sheriff nodded and we went to work, located the breaker box and all lights were soon off.

Investigator Jason Kennedy called the suspect on the phone. The negotiation went on for at least forty-five minutes, and finally Pearlman surrendered.

I advised Kennedy and Ferrell to transport the suspect to the Sheriff's Office. Kennedy had built a rapport with Pearlman, but I still didn't want him to be alone with the suspect.

This somber case has yet to go to trial, so I am not at liberty to release the evidence.

Chapter Forty

Not everything that we have to deal with as law enforcement officers, thank God, is negative. Once in a while there is an incident which helps us to see that we are there for those who need us at the most opportune moment. Such a heartwarming story is that of Detective Dale Stone on Monday afternoon, March 14, 2011.

Dale was the first of several officers dispatched to the Cedar Lane Apartment complex to investigate a report that a three-year-old boy was choking on a hotdog. When Dale arrived at the home, he found the child limp and lifeless, and not breathing. Immediately, he checked and discovered that the boy had no pulse.

Stone began CPR techniques at once. It became apparent that there was an obstruction still remaining in the child's throat. After several attempts, Stone was able to dislodge the visible piece of the hotdog and continued CPR. In only moments, the boy began breathing, coughing and crying, but after only a few breaths, he fell unconscious once again. Remaining calm, Stone called an ambulance.

It was obvious to the other officers that Stone was doing everything possible to resolve the situation.

As soon as the paramedics arrived, while a pressing crowd looked on, they were able to utilize advanced techniques to clear the remaining obstruction from the toddler's throat, and once again revive him.

The child was rushed to Harton Medical Center where he was examined and soon released.

The Tullahoma Sunday News stated, "'Police officers, bystanders and EMS personnel were interviewed and all stated that without the actions of Detective Stone, the outcome of the incident would have most likely been fatal,' Blackwell said."

Dale humbly told them, "I just did what anybody would have done." He further stated that having a child of his own made him, "just act."

I am very proud of the job that Dale and all of my officers do, and will miss being with them on a daily basis.

Chapter Forty-one

On Monday evening, June 6, 2011, Joe and Ruth Wells met Linda and me at Fast Jack's for dinner. We have been doing this for the past five years. We used to meet at the American Legion before it closed.

Linda had been preparing for a hike with her sister, Joan Chatham, and Chuck Lawson, through the Smokies.

The plan was to take two vehicles, leave one at Newport, Standing Bear Hostel, in East Tennessee, and drive the other to Gatlinburg on Sunday, June 12th, and stay at a hotel there Sunday night. I was to have breakfast with Linda, Joan and Chuck, then drop them off at a trailhead to Mount Le Conte, and then I was to drive back home. They were to climb Mount Le Conte, and hike from there back to Newport. All of this was to take an entire week, with them staying in shelters at night. Their adventure was to end on Saturday, the 18th, and then it was their aim to drive back late that evening.

While we were having dinner on Monday, Linda and Ruth were busily engaged in conversation while Joe and I were reflecting on our past experiences in law enforcement.

Reflections of an Investigator

Joe was on duty in Memphis on Thursday evening, April 4th, 1968, when Martin Luther King was assassinated. He was relating the details of this sad experience to me that night. Somehow the conversation shifted to being ready when life came to an end. Maybe it was thinking about King's sudden and unexpected death, I don't know. Joe said he didn't mind dying; he just didn't want to be in any pain.

We didn't get together the next Monday because Linda was on her hike.

Joe called me on Wednesday and asked me if I would have dinner with him and Ruth that evening at Fast Jack's. My sister, however, had already asked me to have dinner with her family, and I had accepted, so I politely declined.

Joe and Ruth went to Fast Jack's that evening by themselves, and had just gotten back home. Joe had taken maybe two steps when he fell face down on the ground.

Frantically, Ruth called 911. The paramedics arrived shortly and took Joe to the E.R. at Harton, then directly to ICU. Joe passed away the next day, Thursday, June 16th, 2011. Linda got home on Saturday about 9:00 P.M.

We went to see Ruth on Sunday afternoon, and the funeral was held on Monday. Joe's talk with me seemed eerily prophetic—a bit like Dr. King's "I Have a Dream" speech. He didn't suffer a lot of pain. He was a great man, and a wonderful friend.

Lorraine Motel in Memphis where Dr. King was assassinated on April 4th, 1968

Chapter Forty-two

One warm Saturday morning in August of 2011 I was sitting at home at the dining table alone, sipping coffee and reminiscing on my career and incidents which I would include in this memoir. My thoughts settled on a day much like this one. Eighteen years had passed, but the memories were still embedded in my mind like initials carved in a colossal oak.

It was late summer of 1993. At that time I lived just outside of the city of Tullahoma on Fran and Dan Marcum's farm, and I helped out with the chores— George and I—George worked for the Marcum's, too. I was a detective, of course, with the Department. Anyhow, George and I were moving the cows up to the field near the barn because the next day the vet was coming to check them out. I was down by the creek and George was further up the hill. I had gotten out of breath and had to stop. After I rested a bit I walked on up the hill. By the time I caught up with George I was short of breath again.

"What's wrong with you, boy?" George said, a worried look on his face.

"I don't know," I answered, "just tired, I guess."

We got the cows watered and fed so they would hang around the barn. I went on home, and when I got there, my daughter wanted me to walk down to the lake with her. On the way back up from our stroll, I had to stop to rest again, so I told my daughter to go on to the house and I would be along soon. By the time I got back to the house I was exhausted.

I sat in my recliner for about an hour while my daughter fixed supper. It was Wednesday, and we usually went to church after our evening meal that night. I told my daughter to go on to church, since the two of us were there alone, as I didn't feel well, and was going to get some rest. When she got home from church I was feeling a bit better, and went on to bed.

The following day I went on to work. As the day wore on, I began feeling worse, so I called my doctor at the VA Hospital and she told me to come in ASAP. When I got to her office, she did an exam and had a bunch of tests done, one of which was a stress test. Immediately she had me admitted to the Intensive Care Unit.

"What is going on?" I asked her.

"Ron, you're on the verge of having a heart attack," she said—not what I wanted to hear.

The nurse brought me a phone and let me call my daughter. Then they did an arteriogram. The next day I had triple-bypass surgery, and three days later when I awakened I was still in recovery.

It was three months before I was able to return to work. Next to the experience I had endured when my life was almost taken by conspirators, this was the most traumatic time in my life. I never dreamed that anything could be so painful. I had thought that I would die in my line of duty as a law enforcement officer, not of a heart problem. It took a lot out of me. It was very difficult to make a comeback, but with the help of God, family and friends, as well as the entire police department and the city behind me, I survived once again.

Then, in mid-summer of 2006, I was driving home from work one day. I was waiting for a traffic light to change at the corner of East Lincoln and Anderson Streets when all of a sudden I heard a crash and saw a van come sliding sideways at my vehicle—my detective unit. It slammed into the side of my unit, totaling it! The next thing I remember, my wife and Lieutenant Higginbotham were helping the paramedics get me into an ambulance. I was rushed to the E.R. at Harton Hospital, treated and released into the able hands of my wife, Linda, who drove me home. That time I was out for a couple of days before returning to work.

The following Friday, my wife and I were having dinner at the American Legion with our friends, Chuck and Fran Lawson, and Joe Wells, whose death I just told you about, and his wife, Ruth. About half way through the meal, I told Linda to take me home, I wasn't feeling well. When we got there, I went and lay down on the bed. The pain was almost unbearable—I couldn't even call for my wife. After a short time, Linda came back into the room. I was sweating and cold at the same time. Linda gave me one of my nitroglycerine pills, and the pain subsided after about five minutes, and so Linda went upstairs to watch TV. About thirty minutes alter, the pain came back. This time I was able to call Linda, so she ran downstairs and gave me another nitro pill. Once again, the pain was subdued, and I told her that I was going to bed for the night.

A third time, this same scenario occurred. Since my wife is a registered nurse, she agreed to administer one more nitro, but told me that if the pain didn't go away for good this time, she was going to call 911. It didn't go away. The ambulance arrived and I was whisked away to the E.R. at Harton. The diagnosis: I had had a full-blown heart attack. I was taken immediately to Vanderbilt Hospital in

Nashville. After four stints and two weeks later, I was sent back home. On Saturday, my daughter, Shannon, was there, as was Investigator Jason Ferrell and his father, J.C. Ferrell, who was Chief of Police at the time, working on my charge. My wife, who was the Director of the E.R. at Harton was at work. I started having pains, and my daughter went outside and got Jason and his dad. When they came back in, they called 911, and again, an ambulance came and took me to the E.R. at Harton. I spent another two weeks there, until my heart made its own bypass, and was again sent home. Once more, I had survived a difficult episode.

Again, God, family, friends and the Department helped me through. My pastor, Herb Hester, and his staff came to see me every day, and the whole church and community prayed and I was soon well enough to return to work.

Then again, in 2008, I had another heart attack and was in the hospital and at home for a while before returning to work. It is 2011, and I am still working.

I could not have made it without the support of God and my church and its wonderful leader/pastor, Herb Hester, my beautiful and wonderful wife, Linda, and my lovely daughters, Shannon, Leah, and Yolanda, "Daddy's girls," and for them, I am forever thankful.

Reflections of an Investigator

And so it is with great hope—hoping that my cool bravado masks my inner grief as I write my letter of retirement—that I realize I will soon be facing life without my "badge."

Chapter Forty-three

There are some pensive facts which I wish to impart before concluding this book. A significant element of law enforcement work is the fact that you experience situations which are obviously very unfair. The most startling example of this is when someone dies as a result of the capricious actions of another. In such cases you feel incredible anger and enormous frustration. It just makes you want to set things right. You witness moments when families are latterly ripped apart—when loved ones die senselessly. By virtue of your position as an investigator, you are expected to be detached and unbiased, and expected to take the appropriate actions according to the law.

The death of any innocent person is horrible, but when it happens to a child, the atrocity of the crime is compounded ten fold.

During my tenure of law enforcement I have seen numerous death situations, from simple accidents to ruthless homicides. Natural, accidental, homicidal and suicidal are four distinctive types of death. There are, however, two other types which must be listed in my line of work—non determined and non-classified. One of these classifications usually occurs when there are too many factors that could have caused a person's demise.

Reflections of an Investigator

I have walked along railroad tracks picking up body parts, looking up under trains for flesh and bones. I've seen heads separated from their bodies. I've viewed the remains of individuals who have taken their own lives with shotguns, rifles and pistols; people who have been crushed in auto accidents, been burned in homes and automobiles to attempt to cover up a homicide. I've seen the victims of hangings and drownings, and babies burnt, beaten and shaken.

One particular incident stands out in my mind. A precious little two-year-old boy was bounced off the walls, shaken and beaten. Needless to say, the baby died. We found his shoes, and there was blood all over them, inside and out. As this beautiful little child lay on the hospital bed there wasn't a dry eye in the E. R. — men and women alike. Even other patients had tears streaming down their cheeks. Six detectives were present, and only two of them would agree to take pictures.

It is scenes like these which break our hearts. Sometimes words are not enough. Only love can help us go on.

Reflections of an Investigator

Chapter Forty-four

On June 1, 2011, I presented the following inter-office memo to Chief Paul Blackwell, a copy going to Mayor Troy Bisby and City Administrator Louis J. Baltz.

I will be retiring after 27 years with the Tullahoma Police Department and therefore December 31, 2011 will be my last day as Investigations Captain.

We have a talented group of law enforcement officers; a group of the greatest, brightest, and most dedicated individuals in the area. Our investigators are professional, hardworking, and up for any task that is assigned to them. I know that each of them will be a shining example in the investigations field. With their direction for the Tullahoma Police Department we will be better equipped and more prepared for the service and protection of our citizens. I have seen several administrators and truly feel we are in a superior position to serve our community.

My choice to retire has been most reluctant and definitely a difficult one. With a much needed focus on easing into Retirement. Therefore, I wish you good fortune and God bless you in your endeavor for better law enforcement.

Sincerely,

[signature: Ron Cunningham]

Captain Ron Cunningham

Pictorial

Ron's favorite hobby — reading

Ron sipping his favorite morning beverage

A younger Ron with friend's daughter

Ron at Normandy Lake

Ron's lovely wife, Linda

Ron as President of Highland Rim Scottish Society speaking at Scottish Burns Dinner

A proud moment at Yolanda's wedding

Daughters Leah and Yolanda

Ron (back right) in Nashville meeting with Governor Phil Bredesen

Ron at a picnic for Police Department

Ron's wolf, Beo, looking at granddaughter, Brylee

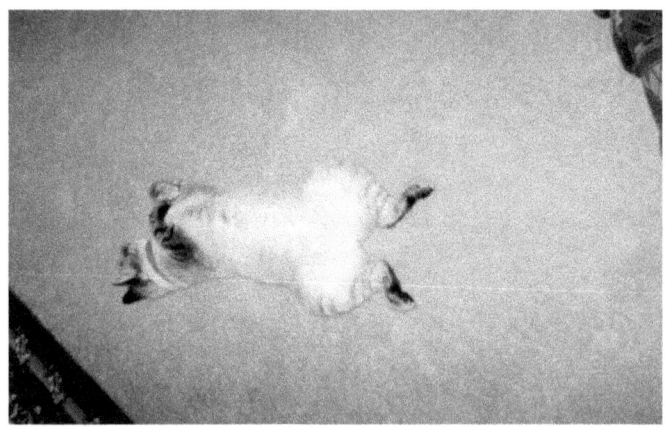

Our cat, O. B. rolls over

Ron with daughter Shannon and girls in Ohio

Ron in 2010 behind his desk

Ron in California at the notorious Alcatraz

Ron climbing ladder in Grand Canyon, Arizona

Ron in Octaltree Scotland under
Clan Cunningham Coat of Arms

Ron and Linda at Highland Rim Scottish Society Burns Dinner

Ron with Clan Cunningham Chief

Ron with friends showing copy of Conspiracy in the Town that Time Forgot

Findlay Castle, Greenock, Scotland where Ron and Linda visited on a recent trip. This was Headquarters for Clan McMillan

Ron at wedding of stepson, Mark Keasling, in Japan

Ron in his tuxedo

Linda by statue in Washington, D.C. of two nurses at the Viet Nam War Women's Memorial

Reflections of an Investigator

History and Origin of the Cunningham Family

The Cunningham family is listed in Douglas Peerage-Volume I, page 632.

Warnebald, the progenitor of this family, settled in Glengarnock, or Cunningham, as a vassal under Hugh DeMorville, constable of Scotland, who died in 1162, and from whom he obtained the manor of Cunningham, which comprised the church and the greater part of the Parish of Kilmaurs. He had turned from a common vassal to a valued leader of Hugh DeMorville's army. From the holdings that he had received, he was given the right to assume the name Cunningham. The ruins of Glengarnock or Cunningham Castle still stands in the edge of the Garnock River two miles north of Kilbirnie, North Ayrshire, Scotland (see photo, page 249). It is uncertain as to when and by whom the castle was erected, but was likely a member of the Cunningham family. The castle was sacked by the Danes in the early history of the clan.

Through the force of arms and general striving, the Cunninghams made themselves one of the foremost families of Scotland. This clan, until recently headed by Sir William Montgomery Cunningham, is still strong and active. Harvey

DeCunningham, Family tradition holds, fought at the Battle of Largs in 1263 and thereby earned a confirmation on the following year from Alexander II.

In 1321, Hugh DeCunningham got lands of Lamburton from Robert the Bruce, and thereafter a series of marriages moved the family ahead. Hugh DeCunnighham's son, Sir William Cunningham, married the heiress of Danly and his grandson, Sir Alexander Cunningham was created Lord of Kilmaurs in or about 1462, and Earl of Glenbairn in 1488. Robert, 2nd Laird of Kilmaurs, was deprived of his father's Earldom, but it was revived for his brother, Cuthbert, 3rd Laird of Kilmaurs. Various members of the Cunningham Clan played parts in exciting and colorful life of Mary, Queen of Scots, and it was that regal lady who lifted one branch of the family into a feudal barony. Alexander Cunningham, 5th Earl of Glencairn, was one of the most prominent and active members of the clan, being one of the promoters of the Reformation of Scotland. He stopped the advance of Mary, Queen of Scots, with a force of 2500 volunteers.

There are two coats of arms registered to the Cunningham family. The oldest, the arms of Glencairn, has the fork and unicorn crests, and the same motto, but instead of coneys, one side has a

Reflections of an Investigator

soldier with a spear and the other side farmer holding a fork.

In connection with the name Cunningham, it was variously spelled as Conynghan, Cuningham, Cuminghame and Cunningham. The old Anglo-Saxon spelling was Conyngham, meaning *King's Home*. The family was prolific and by the time the King of England demanded their allegiance to him as head of the Church of England, their numbers were spread throughout England, Scotland and Ireland. The inhabitants of Scotland were primarily Presbyterians, with a deeply religious character and extremely conscientious. Their material accomplishments as pioneers, adventurers, traders, statesmen, and leaders in literature and finance showed them to be worthy peers of any of the peoples of the world. The Presbyterians of Scotland were persecuted by the English when they refused their allegiance to the King as head of the Church. Their persecution was so great that many of the Scots were tortured and slain under the so-called heresy laws of the time. Thousands immigrated to Northern Ireland, to lands previously devastated by the English. In the mid 1600s and early 1700s many came to America. The first to come settled in the Boston area and those in the 1700s settled in Virginia, and were the ancestors of many of the Cunninghams found all over America today.

The entrance to Glengarnock Castle

Bibliography

Tullahoma City website www.tullahomatn.gov

The Officer Down Memorial Page
http://www.odmp.org/year.php

Wikipedia article, Nurse
http://en.wikipedia.org/wiki/Nurse, references from

Quaker to Catholic, Mary Howitt, the Lost Author of the Nineteenth Century by Joy Dunicliff, St. Clair Publications, UK, USA, © 2010, page 73, reference to Florence Nightingale.

A Soldier of Tennessee, Sam Davis Elliott, LSU Press, 2004 ISBN 978-0-8071-2970-8, reference from

Wikipedia article on Tullahoma, Tennessee, references from
http://en.wikipedia.org/wiki/Tullahoma,_Tennessee

TSLA History of Tennessee Resorts, Springs History, references from

http://www.tennessee.gov/tsla/exhibits/tnresorts/spring_histories.htm, references from

Interview of Stan St. Clair with Johnny Mitchell, Estill Springs, TN, July 9, 2009

http://familytreemaker.genealogy.com/users/j/a/c/Shannon-C-Jackson/WEBSITE-0001/UHP-0264.html John A. Gunn (b. 1765, d. 1853), reference from

State Board of Health Bulletin, Volume 5, November 20, 1889, Nashville, Tennessee, references from

*Historical and Biographical Sketches of Coffee County, Tenn*essee, 1887, Godspeed Publishing, Chicago, IL and Nashville, TN

http://bellsouthpwp.net/C/a/CanCofHist/coffee/goodcoff.htm , reference from

Manchester Tennessee web site article on triple homicide at http://www.manchester-tennessee.com

WRRN TV story Channel 2, Nashville, Tennessee, September 2010

The *Tullahoma News*, Friday, December 19, 1997, article, "750,000 bond is set in multiple rape case."

The *Tullahoma News*. Undated article "Police say eight arrests solve 31 auto burglaries."

The *Tullahoma News*, Undated articles, "Six youths arrested after Tullahoma gang shootings." and

"Teen gang members try two robberies, shoot at victims, rake housing area."

Wikipedia Article, "Dungeons and Dragons," http://en.wikipedia.org/wiki/Dungeons_%26_Dragons

The *Tullahoma News*, Undated article. "Granddaughter charged in Internet romance case."

Tullahoma Police Department official public records, case of the murder and arson at 604 E. Grizzard St. December 2000, including all attached files, interviews, statements, etc.

Undated related article from *Tullahoma News*, "(Grant) pleads 'not guilty.'"

Undated article from *Tullahoma News*, "Moore Man arrested on robbery charges."

Undated article from *Tullahoma News*, "Man charged in theft of drugs from hospital."

Undated picture from *Tullahoma News*, "Good Feelings at City Hall."

Tullahoma Police Department official public records, case of the case involving the men called 'Harold Buchannan,' and 'Gerald Nesmith' in June

Reflections of an Investigator

and July, 2005, including statements by all parties concerned

Tullahoma Police Department official public records, case of the murder and arson at 203 E. Blackwell St. October 2006, including statements by all parties concerned

Article from *Tullahoma News* dated January 21, 2007, "State civil suit charges "Hackberry" Energy with breaking consumer laws."

Tullahoma Police Department official public records, case of Aggravated Assault at "Last Stop" Bar, 410 E. Warren St. Tullahoma, Tennessee, with all interviews and records, February 1, 2007

Coffee County Sheriff's Department arrest records above assault case

Request for medical records from Harton Hospital and Vanderbilt Hospital in above assault case

Request to set hearing for Beer Board Complaint against bar then located at 410 E. Warren St. Tullahoma, Tennessee, and attached event log

Article from *Tullahoma News* dated Friday, January 11, 2008 Police seek vandals spray-painting 'MK' Graffiti letters across town

Undated articles from *Tullahoma News* "Dynamite found behind attorney's law office" and "Dynamite found at attorney's office not part of a bomb."

Tullahoma Police Department official public records, case of MK graffiti vandalism, with all interviews, records and reports attached.

2006, 2007 Vandalism reports from the city of Tullahoma, Tennessee

Article from *Tullahoma News* dated Wednesday March 17, 1999, "Worth workers charged in thefts."

Article from *Tullahoma News* dated Friday, December 12, 2008, "Eight arrested for alleged sale of cocaine."

Article from *Tullahoma News* dated Wednesday, January 28, 2009, "Man fatally shot by deputies in I-24 chase."

Article from *Tullahoma News* dated Wednesday, January 28, 2009, "5 face charges in THS drug search."

Tullahoma Police Department official public records, case of Solicitation of Aggravated Statutory Rape, and official Criminal Circuit Court Records from July 29, 2009, with all interviews, and reports attached

Article from *Tullahoma News* dated Friday September 24, 2010, "Soldier arrested in triple murder."

Wikipedia article on Assassination of Dr. Martin Luther King at: http://en.wikipedia.org/wiki/Assassination_of_Martin_Luther_King,_Jr.

Notes by Ron Cunningham regarding his personal experiences as a detective with the Tullahoma Police Department

Official Tullahoma Police Department press release and article from *Tullahoma Sunday News*, March 19, 2011, regarding child choking on hotdog saved by Detective Dale Stone

www.ingramcontent.com/pod-product-compliance
Lightning Source LLC
Chambersburg PA
CBHW062157080426
42734CB00010B/1720